EXPLORING CAREERS ON CRUISE SHIPS

Exploring Careers
On Cruise Ships

By
Don Kennedy

The Rosen Publishing Group, Inc.
New York

Published in 1993 by The Rosen Publishing Group, Inc.
29 East 21st Street, New York, NY 10010

Copyright 1993 by Don Kennedy

All rights reserved. No part of this book may be reproduced in any form without permission in writing from the publisher, except by a reviewer.

First Edition

Library of Congress Cataloging-in-Publication Data

Kennedy, Don.
    Exploring careers on cruise ships / by Don Kennedy.—1st ed.
      p.   cm.
    Includes bibliographical references and index.
      Summary: Presents an overview of the jobs available on a cruise ship and discusses the necessary qualifications and skills, wages, benefits, and where and how to apply for a job.
      ISBN 0-8239-1665-0   ISBN 0-8239-1714-2 (pbk)
      1. Cruise ships—Vocational guidance—United States—Juvenile literature. 2. Cruise ships—United States—Job descriptions—Juvenile literature. [1. Cruise ships—Vocational guidance. 2. Vocational guidance.] I. Title.
HE566.E9K458 1993
385'.22'02373—dc20   93-20293
                                                                       CIP
                                                                        AC

Manufactured in the United States of America

To
Granddaddy Wildes,
who wrote and published his second book at age eighty-three, and Grandaddy Kennedy without whose support I couldn't have continued.

Acknowledgments

Special thanks to . . .

My mother, for having faith in me while I tried all these entrepreneurial ideas instead of pursuing something a little more secure.

My father, for getting me hooked on books at age fifteen.

The rest of my family, for their assistance in mailing out thousands of brochures to colleges all over the country, and for their support along the way.

Ammie, for all those hours stuffing envelopes, writing addresses, and keeping me up when I got down.

Mark Bebensee at The Citadel, for helping me put that first résumé together.

Juliann Pugh, Amy Dorn, and Suzanne Kelley for supplying stories for the book and for staying in touch so long after we got off the ships.

Karen, Howard, and the rest of the staff at The Cruise Authority in Atlanta, for supplying me with brochures and answering all my questions.

Mrs. Jesse Bird, my high school English teacher, for inspiring me to do something great and for editing my first draft.

Jennifer, Trish, Rosemary, and the rest of the staff at The Stratford, for letting me use the computer more than the rest of the residents combined.

Acknowledgments

Aly Bello at Carnival, Carol Priest at NCL, Kurt Mackie at Royal Caribbean, and Barbara Weiner at Diana M. Orban Associates for their generosity in supplying pictures and other information essential to the accuracy and scope of this book.

About the Author

Don Kennedy became interested in working aboard cruise ships when, at age seventeen, he took a "senior cruise" with other members of his high school graduating class. Having worked as a disc jockey at a local radio station and having done parties with his own portable system while in high school, he became interested in how the ship's DJ had gotten his job. After questioning him and several other members of the crew, he found that most had simply written and applied!

Early in his freshman year at The Citadel, The Military College of South Carolina, he had begun to consider what he would do during his summer break. With the help of a professor, he organized his first résumé. Then, using a list of cruise line addresses, he began sending out applications.

He kept applying throughout the spring, but by the end of the school year he still had heard nothing. A week after returning home to work for his father, however, he received a phone call from a contractor for Norwegian Cruise Line offering him a job as a DJ on one of their ships.

He spent that summer doing seven-day cruises in the Caribbean aboard the M/S *Starward*. The next two summers he got jobs cruising to Canada and Alaska with Sitmar Cruise Lines and to the Caribbean with Carnival Cruise Lines. Upon graduation from college, he was hired as a purser for Royal Caribbean Cruise Lines.

He worked on board for several months before moving to Atlanta and writing his first book on cruising, *How to Get a Job on a Cruise Ship*.

Contents

	Foreword	xi
1.	What Is a Cruise Ship?	1
2.	The Cruise Industry—An Overview	23
3.	The Job Market	37
4.	What It Takes—Qualifications and Skills	43
5.	Positions Available	55
6.	Who's Hiring?—Where to Apply	67
7.	How to Apply	105
8.	How to Follow Up	115
9.	Interviewing for the Job	121
10.	Preparing to Go	129
11.	Life on Board	138
12.	Is It the Right Job for You?	144
	Appendixes	
	A. *Cruise Ship Ports Around the World*	149
	B. *Answers to Commonly Asked Questions About Cruise Vacations*	156
	Glossary	166
	For Further Reading	169
	Index	171

Foreword

How would you describe the perfect job? One that had so many benefits that it seemed too good to be true? Would it pay you to travel to the most beautiful places in the world? Would it provide you with a free place to live and all the food you could eat? Would it bring you into contact with upscale people from all over the world? Would it entertain you with exciting activities around the clock?

Could a job like that actually exist in today's economy and overcrowded job market?

The answer is—YES! And as you may have guessed from the title of this book, the dream job, or jobs, I am describing can be found aboard a cruise ship. In fact, a cruise ship provides all the benefits described above, and more.

I can say from working on ships of four cruise lines that it is one of the most wonderful job experiences a person could possibly have. There are few others that give a person in his or her twenties the opportunity to visit countries all over the world. There are few, if any, jobs that offer an employee gourmet food—steak, shrimp, lobster, and other delicacies. There is also the opportunity to meet people, both passengers and crew, from all over the world.

It is an eye-opening experience, especially for someone who hasn't traveled much. Coming from a small rural town in the South, I saw and experienced much that was new to me. I was introduced to people of every race, religion, and culture.

If you are seeking a fun—but work required—way to

Foreword

get away for a while, or if you are looking for a career in the travel industry, working on a ship may be the right job for you. If you want to experience and be around the finer things in life, this may be the right job for you. If you enjoy people and would like to meet natives of countries around the world, read on.

Keep in mind that you will be applying for a job. You will have the opportunity to see places and to enjoy yourself, but your purpose in being on the ship is to work. Forget that purpose and get carried away having fun, and you'll end up terminated and right back on land. Make the most of your job, however, enjoy it and do it well, and working on a cruise ship will be one of the most memorable experiences of your life.

Looking at my three volumes of pictures brings back a flood of memories—of sunset dinners overlooking the ocean, hours of snorkeling in crystal-clear waters, and sharing those experiences with friends I had met only the day before.

I have cruised as a passenger now, but it is not the same. When you are a crew member, the other crew members are your family. Within a month of working and living closely with them, you feel that you have known them all your life. I miss the camaraderie. I hope this book will help you get aboard a cruise ship and become a member of your own family at sea.

Don Kennedy

Foreword

The M.S. Seaward of Norwegian Cruise Line sails out of its home port, Miami.

1

What Is a Cruise Ship?

In 1975, television producer Douglas S. Cramer came up with an idea for a comedy television series. The setting would be a luxury cruise ship, and the stars would be members of the ship's crew—the captain, the cruise director, the doctor, a purser, and a bartender. Cramer teamed up on the idea with producer Aaron Spelling, and the series went on to become a major success that ran for nine years.

Princess Cruises had four of its ships (*Royal*, *Island*, *Pacific*, and *Sky*) used as locations for the pilot and subsequent shows. The line became a household word and benefited greatly from the related publicity. It continues today to promote its ships as "the Love Boats," and the TV Captain, Gavin MacLeod, is the company spokesperson.

Many aspects of the show gave viewers a real sense of what it's like to be a passenger and a crew member on a cruise ship. The sense of excitement as the ship left port, the family atmosphere that existed among the crew members, and the ease with which one could develop a serious romantic relationship with someone on the ship were portrayed very realistically.

Other aspects of the show, however, were stretched a bit for dramatic and entertainment purposes. For instance, on a real ship not all of the crew would have been Americans. The captain might have been Norwegian, Italian, or Greek. The cruise director probably would have been American, but the doctor might have been from Sweden, the purser from England, and the bartender from Jamaica. In real life, cruise lines purposely hire a culturally diverse crew to create an international air of excitement on board their ships. Other differences you might have noticed: the captain on a real ship does not wear shorts, he does not hang around the bar talking to the bartenders, and his daughter would not be living on the ship.

The main difference immediately apparent to anyone who has ever taken a cruise was the size of the cabins. On "The Love Boat" the cabins were the size of a normal bedroom. On a real ship not even a master suite would be that big. The cabins are small! That doesn't really matter, of course, since when you sail on a real ship you spend very little time in your cabin. But

Star of "The Love Boat": the Pacific Princess *of Princess Cruise Lines.*

What Is a Cruise Ship?

the most frequent complaint crew members hear from passengers is that they thought the cabins would be larger.

In recent years the cruise lines have begun to use TV for much more of their advertising, allowing people who have thought about taking a cruise to see what a real ship looks like. The commercials usually focus on the variety of activities available, from sunbathing to watersports to eating. Carnival Cruise Lines, through its TV commercials with spokesperson Kathy Lee Gifford ("Live with Regis and Kathy Lee"), have probably done more than anyone to communicate the glamour and excitement that one can expect to find on a cruise ship.

The modern cruise industry as seen in those commercials is only about twenty-five years old. Before that, cruising was simply a way to get from one point to another—across the Atlantic, for example. The increased use of jet aircraft after World War II made slower transportation by ship inefficient, and the passenger industry declined rapidly until the 1960s. Then several innovative companies began tapping the public demand for unique multidestination travel vacations, and cruise ships were transformed from mere transportation into luxurious floating resorts.

Types of Cruises

Many people who are thinking of working on a ship want to know how long they'll be at sea. That varies because cruises have been designed to satisfy everyone from the adventurer seeking an overnight thrill to the retired executive looking to see the world. Here's a brief look at each:

One-day cruises to nowhere. Ships offering this option operate out of several ports in Florida and, to a lesser degree, other ports around the United States. Priced at about $60 to $100, these trips give passengers an overnight of fun and frolic on the high seas. Most ships offer dinner, dancing, entertainment, gambling, and other activities from sunset to sunrise.

Three- and four-day. These cruises primarily serve the Bahamas market. Ships sail out of Miami and Port Canaveral to Nassau, Freeport, and the Bahamas out-islands. Some new ships, such as Carnival's *Fantasy*, have been built specifically for this market. These short cruises are a great way to get out of town for an extended weekend—or to determine if you would like to take a longer cruise.

Seven-day. Many ships serve this market. Most sail to the Caribbean. A seven-day cruise typically allows a ship to visit four or more ports and give the passengers a couple of days at sea. Other options in this category include Mexico and Bermuda.

More than seven days. Cruises from eight to twenty-one days can take you just about anywhere in the world. You may sail from the United State or Canada to Alaska, or from Italy around the Mediterranean. A multitude of destinations are available, and the length of the cruise provides an opportunity to see much of an entire region of the world such as the South Pacific. Of course, the price is much higher than that of a three- or four-day cruise; therefore, experienced cruisers and older, wealthier persons make up the majority of the passengers on these cruises.

World. When a person is ready to see the world in style and can be away from home for a long time, he may choose to sail around the world. On such trips a passenger's cabin becomes his home, and the crew and other passengers his friends. Only a few cruise ships offer this option, because not many people have the time or finances to embark on such a voyage.

WHO TAKES CRUISES?

Many potential cruise passengers have preconceptions about what kind of people take cruises. In some cases, they decide against taking a cruise for fear there will be no one like them on board. In reality, in the past ten years, cruise lines and individual ships have emerged to appeal to every segment of the population, from young to old. No one need be afraid of being the only young single or the only older married couple on board. With a little advice from a travel agent, the right line and ship can be selected to insure that a passenger goes on a cruise with others of the same age group and social status.

	Travel Companions on Most Recent Cruise %
Spouse	58
Friends	34
Other Family Member	10
Children	6
Alone	6

Who takes cruises? The majority are couples, but a large number travel with friends.

Who Might Be Found on Board?

Singles. So many singles take cruises that some companies do nothing but organize these groups to go on cruises. Singles are frequently taking their first or second cruise and opt for shorter vacations of three to seven days, usually in the Caribbean.

The exception is a group who must also be categorized as "singles": elderly women who are sailing alone. They typically choose the more exclusive cruise lines and can afford longer trips. Cruise lines have recognized this category, and more than one have established formal programs providing gentlemen "hosts" to be dining and dancing partners for these ladies.

Honeymooners. A cruise is a great way to spend a honeymoon. A couple can have privacy but also immediate access to other people and entertainment. The setting is extremely romantic and provides ample activities and scenery for a dream honeymoon.

Couples. A cruise is a romantic experience for couples even if they are not newlyweds. Specific cruises cater to married and unmarried couples, young and old. Three-day cruises to the Bahamas or twelve- to fourteen-day grand tours provide a wonderful setting for couples to enjoy a time away from home.

Families. Family cruises are one of the fastest-growing trends in cruising. Recognition of this growth has led the cruise lines to develop programs designed to keep the children actively entertained. Some now employ children's staff year-round; others provide supervision during Christmas and summer breaks. These innovative programs allow parents to take their kids along, yet enjoy some of the freedom of being alone.

WHAT IS A CRUISE SHIP?

WHY PEOPLE TAKE CRUISES

The reasons people take cruises vary widely, of course. But the principal reasons lie in the images generated by TV and the movies and in the advantages cruises offer compared with other vacation options. A few of the most common reasons follow:

There's so much to do. You can participate in sports from dawn to dusk, or you can just sit on deck and do nothing. You can go to a movie, eat at a buffet, shop for perfume, or get a massage all within a two- to three-minute walk of each other. The section later in this chapter, "What's to Do on a Cruise Ship," illustrates how many options are available.

They want to be pampered. This desire ranks at the top of passengers' comment cards on what they enjoyed about their cruise. Few people at home have the luxury of having every meal prepared for them, or their bed turned down, or their clothes hung up. Add to that drinks served to them as they relax at the pool, and it's easy to understand what a desire to be pampered really means.

They want to eat. Up to eleven meals a day make food a main attraction of the cruise experience. And passengers need not feel guilty at enjoying the meals and the resulting effect on their waistline. Cruise lines still offer beautifully arranged spreads, but now with healthy options for those watching their diets. It is also worth noting that the cost of the meals is included in the price of the cruise, so meals can be enjoyed without worrying about paying for them later.

They don't have to pack and unpack. On most land tour vacations, a traveler is caught up in a cycle of unpacking, then repacking at each stop. To get from one city or country to the next, there is a constant rush to catch the next plane, train, or bus. Not so on a cruise ship. A person unpacks once when going aboard, and the ship takes him to each country on the itinerary. This makes for a much less hectic, and therefore more enjoyable, vacation.

The uncommon opportunities. Cruising is an escape from reality. It is an experience that can make one feel rich even if he isn't. It is a chance to enjoy, even for a few days, a life-style of dressing up, eating fine meals, and seeing Broadway-style shows.

They get a lot for the money. This is described in detail in the section, "What Does the Price of a Cruise Include?" It can be said briefly, however, that a vacation that includes airfare, transportation, and all meals, entertainment, and activities is considered a good value by potential and experienced vacationers.

Romance. Anyone who has seen an episode of "The Love Boat" or one of the TV commercials mentioned earlier can conjure up a pretty vivid image of what cruising is like. The pampering, the service, the relaxation, the dressing up, the moonlit nights, the exotic destinations and beautiful scenery create an unmatched romantic experience for anyone sailing with someone special.

WHAT THE PRICE OF A CRUISE INCLUDES

One of a travel agent's most potent sales tools in persuading a client to take a cruise is the value of the vacation dollar compared to that of a similar vacation on land. The following discussion makes it clear that cruises are not as expensive as they're perceived to be. And because they are paid for up front, more time is spent enjoying the vacation than constantly pulling money out of a wallet or cashing travelers checks.

If you were a passenger, what would you be getting for the price of your cruise?

What Is a Cruise Ship?

A room. You don't pay for hotel or resort accommodations by the night as you would on land. Your cabin is your room, and it's paid for as part of the price of the cruise.

Transportation. Traveling to three or four countries in seven days would cost thousands of dollars in airfare alone. Add to that cab fares to and from hotels, porter tips, and car rental, and the total cost of just getting from place to place would be several thousand dollars. On a cruise, however, the ship is your transportation, and you can visit four countries in seven days for a fraction of the cost. Your transportation from place to place is included in the price of the cruise.

Three (plus) meals a day. What do three meals a day for a family of four cost in a hotel or restaurant? A lot! But on a cruise ship you can eat three times that many meals and still not have finished. Everything—from the sunrise coffee and croissant to the elaborate midnight buffet—is included in the price of the cruise.

Entertainment. How much are four tickets to a Broadway-style show every night for a week? Hundreds of dollars. Not so on a cruise ship. You get to choose from an endless variety of entertainment, from a chorus line of dancers to an ensemble of big-band musicians, and it's all part of the price of the cruise.

Dancing. On land you may pay a $10 cover charge to get into a club offering a live band or a DJ playing dance music. On a ship you have access to clubs offering reggae, jazz, piano, or high-energy dance, all without having to drive to them, and all included in the price of the cruise.

Sports and activities. On land if you want to work out or learn to samba, you have to pay for it. On a cruise ship, it's the staff's job to make sure passengers have the option to enjoy these activities and more, and it's all included in the price of the cruise.

The kind of expansive midnight buffet served on board most ships.

WHAT'S TO DO ON A CRUISE SHIP

Boredom is not a problem of passengers on a cruise ship. They may choose not to participate in what's offered but just to relax on deck with a book, but the options are available nonetheless. One of the cruise director's main responsibilities is to make sure that at any given time there is a choice of things for people to do. This includes not only organizing activities, but also making sure that the public areas (spa, open decks, etc.) are being utilized in some structured program for the passengers' entertainment.

Although the following list is quite long, it is by no means exhaustive. The size of the ship, its itinerary, and the ingenuity of the cruise director and his staff will ensure that there is always a variety of things for passengers to do.

Aerobicize. Led by the Fitness Instructor or a dancer, sessions are held inside or on deck. Levels may be available for beginner, advanced, or older adults.

Attend a show. A major event is staged nightly in the ship's main showroom: Broadway-style dance revues, comedians, singers, jugglers, ventriloquists, and others.

Dance. A big band plays a variety of music in the ballrooms, steel bands play calypso on deck, and the disco pulses with high-energy dance music.

Dress up. If the ship has a costume night, people dress in everything from homemade costumes to elaborate outfits rented for the occasion.

Eat. An activity unto itself! Food is available in dazzling displays from before sunrise until after midnight. Many ships offer an endless array of dining options, including first class in the dining room, lunch buffets on deck, à la carte in a supper club, or informal in a pizzeria or ice cream parlor.

Gamble. Try your luck at blackjack, poker, roulette, or the slot machines. On larger ships, the casino may occupy space on two decks and contain hundreds of machines and tables.

Get a massage. Book it through the health club or the beauty salon. Expect to pay an extra charge for this.

Golf. Hit one off the top deck into the ocean, or some ships offer a high-tech simulator of top courses around the world.

Jog. Around the decks or on a machine. Do it on your own or in organized group sessions.

Learn something. Many ships employ lecturers who conduct classes in everything from birdwatching to computer operation.

Play bridge or backgammon. Organized classes and informal get-togethers both provide opportunities to hone your skills.

Play paddle tennis. On deck or in the game room.

Play basketball or volleyball. On deck on some larger ships.

Read. For some people the optimal vacation is just vegetating with a good book. Opportunities abound in the cabin, the public rooms, or in the shade on deck.

Scuba dive. From a special watersports deck on some ships, or arranged in port through the shore excursion director.

See a movie. Some ships show top-run movies, particularly on days at sea. Many have theaters just like those on land. On newer ships, it may be possible to see one on the TV in your cabin.

Shoot some hoops. Basketball courts are available on deck on some larger ships.

Shop till you drop. Possibilities on board range from small gift shops to entire arcades of specialty boutiques.

Show off your talent. The passenger show is an organized excuse for people to display their talents or make complete idiots of themselves. A fun activity for cash and prizes.

Shuffleboard. Usually several courts can be found on deck.

Sightsee. From the deck of a ship there's a lot to see—the fjords of Norway, dolphins swimming alongside, and always beautiful sunrises and sunsets.

Sing along. Many ships have a piano bar where it's possible to request your favorite song and then have everyone sing along.

Sleep. For some, the ideal vacation is rest and relaxation. With the availability of rapid room service, they don't even have to get out of bed to eat.

Snorkel. From the special watersports decks found on a few of the newer ships.

Socialize. The entire time of the cruise provides

endless opportunities to meet people from throughout the United States and the world. Those who are not shy have no problem making new friends or possibly even developing a romantic interest.

Sunbathe. Naturally available on any ship sailing in a warm climate. Deck chairs abound in both crowded areas and quieter, more private ones all over the ship.

Sweat in the sauna. Part of the spa facilities on some larger ships.

Swim. Probably only four or five ships in the world do not have pools. Newer, larger ships have three or four with slides and outdoor hot tubs.

Take pictures. There's no shortage of opportunities for photographs, not only of people, but also of exotic ports and romantic sunsets. And when a personal camera is not available, the ship's photographer is usually there to snap the shot.

Work out. Almost all ships have a workout area. These range from a few universal machines on smaller ships to large gyms with a hundred machines on others.

COMMON MYTHS AND MISCONCEPTIONS ABOUT CRUISING

Knowing the truth about cruise ships and cruising will help you make a more educated decision about whether you want to work on a ship and enable you to help passengers enjoy their cruise more once you're aboard. The following are common myths and misconceptions that passengers have.

Myth #1: I've never been on a cruise. I don't think I would like it.

Fact: Studies show that cruises have the highest satisfaction rating of any type of vacation. That's why so many people who were skeptical when they first boarded a ship come off it committed to taking another

How I Got My Job as a Recreation/Fitness Director

In the winter quarter of my senior year of college, I was graduating with an Exercise Science degree and had had no luck finding a job. I was teaching a water aerobics class to some women in the community; and one of them, having just returned from a cruise, said that classes like mine were taught on the ship and that I would be ideal for the job. Being from the Midwest, I didn't even know the name of a cruise line, but my school adviser had a cousin who worked for Royal Caribbean Cruise Line. That's the line I thought I'd try.

I wrote to this contact, asking whom I should approach about applying. She sent me the name of the RCCL personnel director for the cruise staff. RCCL then sent me an application, which I quickly returned with a 35 mm snapshot for the required photo (I later learned that most applicants sent an 8 × 10 black-and-white glossy with an audition tape).

By Easter, I hadn't heard anything, so I called to confirm that they had received my info. I was told by the person who answered the phone that he received 1,000 applications a month, that he didn't know my name, and that he'd get back to me if interested. I basically gave up at that point.

Months later, on the Sunday of Labor Day weekend, I received a call from RCCL saying that they were sailing Saturday, could I be there on Friday? Needless to say, I jumped at the chance, and I have never once regretted the decision.

Amy Dorn

cruise in the near future. On some ships, over two thirds of the passengers are repeat cruisers. Many passengers don't want to get off at the end of the cruise.

Myth #2: It costs too much.

Fact: A cruise is very affordable and gives you great value for your money compared to other vacations. We have discussed what is included in the price of a cruise. The counter to this myth is simply that cruises don't cost as much as uninformed people think, and what you get for the price makes it well worth it.

Myth #3: I don't know anything about it. It's easier to plan a vacation on land.

Fact: That's where experienced travel agents enter the picture. Their role is discussed in detail in Chapter 2, but basically it is as middleman between the consumer and the cruise line. People wanting to take a cruise just decide where they want to go, and what line they'd like to go on; the travel agent does the rest.

Myth #4: I can't afford plane tickets plus the cost of the cruise.

Fact: No problem. On almost all cruises, air transportation is included in the price. There are also rail options; and if a person lives close enough to drive, the price of the airfare is subtracted.

Myth #5: I don't want to book months in advance. I plan my vacations at the last minute.

Fact: Although it is easier to get the particular cabin, dining room sitting, and other preferred options when a cruise is booked early, many ships have space available even up to sailing time, because of cancellations.

Myth #6: I can't go on a cruise out of the country because I don't have a passport.

Fact: That is not likely to be necessary. When sailing out of a U.S. home port, one needs only a driver's license and a copy of a birth certificate. When the ship is docked in a foreign port, usually only a room key or a boarding pass has to be shown to get on and off the ship.

Myth #7: I don't want to play bingo and participate in all those activities. I just want to relax at my own pace.

Fact: Fine. None of the organized activities are mandatory. It's the passenger's choice whether to play deck games or just lie on the deck. On most ships the only regularly scheduled activity is dinner. A few luxury ships are not even that structured, and passengers can eat whenever they like.

Myth #8: I don't have a tuxedo or gown for the formal nights.

Fact: On 90 percent of ships, jacket and tie for men is acceptable, and may even be the norm, for formal nights. Women wear evening or cocktail dresses. A few upscale lines do require a tuxedo or elegant gown, but chances are, people who can afford one of these cruises already own the appropriate attire.

Myth #9: I heard you have to sleep in bunkbeds.

Fact: There are not bunkbeds in the cabins, but the beds that fold out of the ceiling may make it seem so. Fold-down beds are seldom found when there are only two people in a cabin; they are used almost exclusively when there are three and four in a cabin.

WHAT IS A CRUISE SHIP?

Myth #10: It's too crowded on board.

Fact: It's true that some of the newer ships carry more than 1,500 passengers, but those are certainly not the only option available. In fact, a major trend in the industry is toward smaller, more yacht-like vessels. These may carry fewer than a hundred passengers and probably few if any children. They specialize in an unstructured environment and peace and quiet.

Myth #11: I don't want to have nights when I have to dress a certain way.

Fact: Then you may want to consider the smaller, more relaxed cruise lines that offer more of a back-to-nature cruise or aim to educate you, not endlessly entertain you. There is no required attire for these cruises. One line even promotes its casual atmosphere with the slogan, "Barefoot Cruises."

Myth #12: There's nothing but foreign people on board.

Fact: That may be true on cruises from and to only non-U.S. ports—a cruise in the Mediterranean or along the coasts of China and Japan, for instance. But the overwhelming majority of cruise passengers are from North America, which means there's a good chance they speak fluent English and share American customs. True, most of the crew on a ship are not from the U.S., but that is one of the hidden benefits of working on board.

Myth #13: I don't want to just go to the Caribbean.

Fact: Although over half of all cruises do go to the Caribbean, many don't. A person can visit the Amazon River in South America, tour the old cities of Italy in the Mediterranean, explore the mysteries of the Far

17

East, or reach out and touch a glacier in Alaska. As more and more people cruise, they seek new destinations. The cruise lines are continually innovating to meet that demand with itineraries including new continents, off-the-beaten-path foreign ports, and their own private islands.

Myth #14: I don't have anyone to go with me.

Fact: That really isn't a problem, for two reasons. One, most lines have programs for pairing up single cruisers in a cabin. "Single" in this case doesn't mean unmarried, but those sailing alone in need of a roommate. Second, there are companies such as Singleworld that as part of their program offerings pair roommates together. It is possible to be the only person in a cabin, but most lines charge one and a half or two times the regular fare for this luxury.

Myth #15: There's nothing to do but lie on deck or sightsee.

Fact: The previous section illustrates the fact that there is no shortage of things to do on a ship. In the past ten years, cruise lines have made great strides in building facilities and organizing activities to entertain passengers from dawn till dusk. Boredom need not be a worry for any potential cruiser.

Myth #16: I'll get fat if I eat all that food.

Fact: Not any more! In response to the continuing trend toward better health, the cruise lines have established a variety of dietary options to help passengers take in less, plus numerous fitness activities to help them take off more. Menu options have such names such as Lite Cuisine, Heartsmart Selections, and

WHAT IS A CRUISE SHIP?

SEABOURN
HERALD

GOOD MORNING

9:00 a.m.	Morning Wake up and Stretch Class in the Spa.
10:00 a.m.	Today's Quiz available in the library (answers given at afternnoon tea).
10:00 a.m.	Bridge Lecture in the Card Room.
11:00 a.m.	Enrichment Lecture: "Brasil Today" with Ambassador Per Proitz Amundsen Lounge.
12:00 noon	Nautical Information from the Bridge.

GOOD AFTERNOON

2:30 p.m.	Bridge game in the Card Room.
2:30 p.m.	Meet partners for games, scrabble etc. The Social Staff will make introductions in the Horizon Lounge.
3:30 p.m.	Fitness class in the Spa. Low impact Aerobics and Body Conditioning.
4:00 p.m.	Recorded concert hour. "Great Classical Marches," in the Horizon Room.
4:00 p.m.	Port Briefing on Salvador (Bahia) by Travel Manager Scott in the Amundsen Lounge (this can also be seen on TV channel #3 in your suite).

GOOD EVENING

7:00-8:30 p.m.	Glyn Baily plays during coctails in the Club.
7:00-8:30 p.m.	Music for dancing or listening pleasure with the Jerry Blaine Quartet in the Amundsen Lounge.
7:30 p.m.	Cocktail Fashions, presented by Oyevind Brundtland from the Boutique, in the Amundsen Lounge.
9:45 p.m.-Midnight	Come dance to the Jerry Blaine Quartet in the Amundsen Lounge.
10:00 p.m.-close	Glyn Baily entertains at he piano in the Club.

☆ ☆ ☆ SHOWTIME ☆ ☆ ☆

10:15 p.m.	Featuring an evening with Todd Petersen in the Amundsen Lounge.

There's always something for passengers to do, even on upscale ships with fewer scheduled activities.

ShipShape items. All offer food choices that are low in cholesterol, fat, and sodium; there may also be vegetarian or kosher fare.

Myth #17: I'll get seasick.

Fact: That could happen, but it's doubtful. Most cruise ships sail in smooth seas and are equipped with stabilizers to handle any rough seas that may be encountered. Also, the Purser's Desk typically offers free sickness prevention tablets to those concerned.

Myth #18: I don't have time to take a cruise.

Fact: As discussed earlier in the chapter, cruise lines now offer a host of new options. One-day cruises to nowhere sail from various ports around the U.S., and three- and four-day cruises hit the best of the Bahamas. All allow a quick getaway from work plus an inexpensive way to sample the cruise experience.

Myth #19: There's nothing for my kids to do.

Fact: Another trend in the cruise industry is the number of parents taking young children along on vacations. Almost all lines catering to the twenty-five- to forty-five-year-old segment of the population have instituted brand-name kids' programs to keep the children entertained and their parents stress-free. Almost all of these ships employ children's counselors or youth coordinators during the summer and at Christmas. Many of the larger ones keep staff year-round and have nurseries, activity centers, and video arcades for kids from two up.

Myth #20: Cruises are only for rich, elderly people.

Fact: There may have been some truth to that in the old days of cruising and when the modern industry began, but it's no longer true. Cruises vary in length from overnight to three months, and typically the length of the cruise determines the average age and income level of the passengers. Cruises from three days to a week usually cater to the under-fifty-five crowd—students, singles, young married couples, and beginning

WHAT IS A CRUISE SHIP?

families. Longer cruises, ten days and up, usually have older, wealthier passengers, many having already taken several cruises.

Myth #21: There's not enough time in port.

Fact: This may be the only legitimate concern. It is true that cruise ships typically spend less than a day in most ports. But for those wishing to spend more time in one place, there are ships that offer overnight stays in some ports, Bermuda for example; and virtually all lines offer optional land/tour packages before and after the cruise.

A Typical Day as a Disc Jockey

On most ships, as a DJ, you've got it easy. You may not be making as much as some other crew members, but you also aren't working as many hours.

Typically, the ship's disco is open from 10 p.m. to 3 a.m. The DJ, of course, operates the disco. Your presence is required during those hours primarily to play music for dancing. Beyond that, however, you may have the rest of the time off to enjoy the ship as a passenger.

Whether you're so lucky depends on the policies of your cruise line and possibly on the needs of your Cruise Director. As a member of the staff, you may be called upon to assist the Cruise Director with other duties during the day. On one ship, I ran the library for three hours during full days at sea. On another, I helped emcee events and supervise skeet shooting.

On frequent occasions you will be needed to play music for cocktail parties or special games or events on deck. Knowledge and a library of a wide range of music helps. The ship will have its own library, but it can help to bring your own favorites.

Prepare for your natural timeclock to be turned around unless you are accustomed to playing in clubs late at night. "Starting" work at 10 p.m. is nice, since it gives you all day off, but if can also be a lonely job since most of the other crew members are just getting off work and going out to "play."

Don Kennedy

2

The Cruise Industry—An Overview

As I discussed in Chapter 1 and will discuss further in Chapter 9, knowing something about cruises, cruise passengers, and the cruise industry will be an asset to you in your job search. Following is a collection of basic facts, statistics, and trivia that will give you a broad overview and general understanding of the industry.

- The industry keeps growing. Since 1970, the cruise industry has expanded at the rate of 10 percent a year. In response, the cruise lines keep introducing new ships (creating a need for more crew members to staff them).
- Taking a cruise is a dream of nearly 60 percent of all American adults, yet only about 5 percent of the population has ever done so.
- A cruise has the highest satisfaction rating of any type of vacation. That means that people had more fun on their cruise than on any other type of vacation they have taken.
- Over 55 percent of all cruise passengers sail to the Caribbean, visiting ports from Cozumel, Mexico, in the west to Bridgetown, Barbados, in the east.
- The average length of a cruise is six days. This is

decreasing, however, as people with less time are taking cruises of two to five days.
- Most people go on a cruise with their family, but one third of all cruise passengers go with friends.
- Of all comments by passengers to describe their cruise vacation, "pampered by the staff" and "fun" are the two most common.
- Some 91 percent of people who have taken a cruise recently indicate a desire to take another one.
- On a typical ten-day cruise, 1,000 passengers on average consume about 3,000 pounds of cheese, over 35,000 eggs, 500 bottles of champagne, over 1,500 bottles of wine, almost 3,000 cans of beer, over 11,000 pounds of meat, about 21,000 pounds of fresh fruit, 22,000 pounds of vegetables, over a thousand gallons of milk, 12,000 pounds of fish and lobster, 2,000 pounds of pasta, over 3,000 pounds of coffee and sugar, and almost 90,000 loaves of bread, rolls, and breadsticks.
- Cruise ships are often christened by famous people. Among Princess Cruise Line's ships, the *Royal Princess* was christened by Princess Diana; the *Star Princess*, by actress Audrey Hepburn; the *Crown Princess*, by actress Sophia Loren, and the *Regal Princess* by former British Prime Minister Margaret Thatcher.
- Desalination plants aboard a ship produce 400 to 500 tons of water each day for drinking, cooking, and laundry.
- Passengers on a cruise ship have the opportunity to enjoy eleven meals and snacks a day, as well as twenty-four-hour room service.
- It takes between fifty and a hundred tons of water to fill a typical shipboard swimming pool.
- During the Broadway-style shows staged on most

THE CRUISE INDUSTRY—AN OVERVIEW

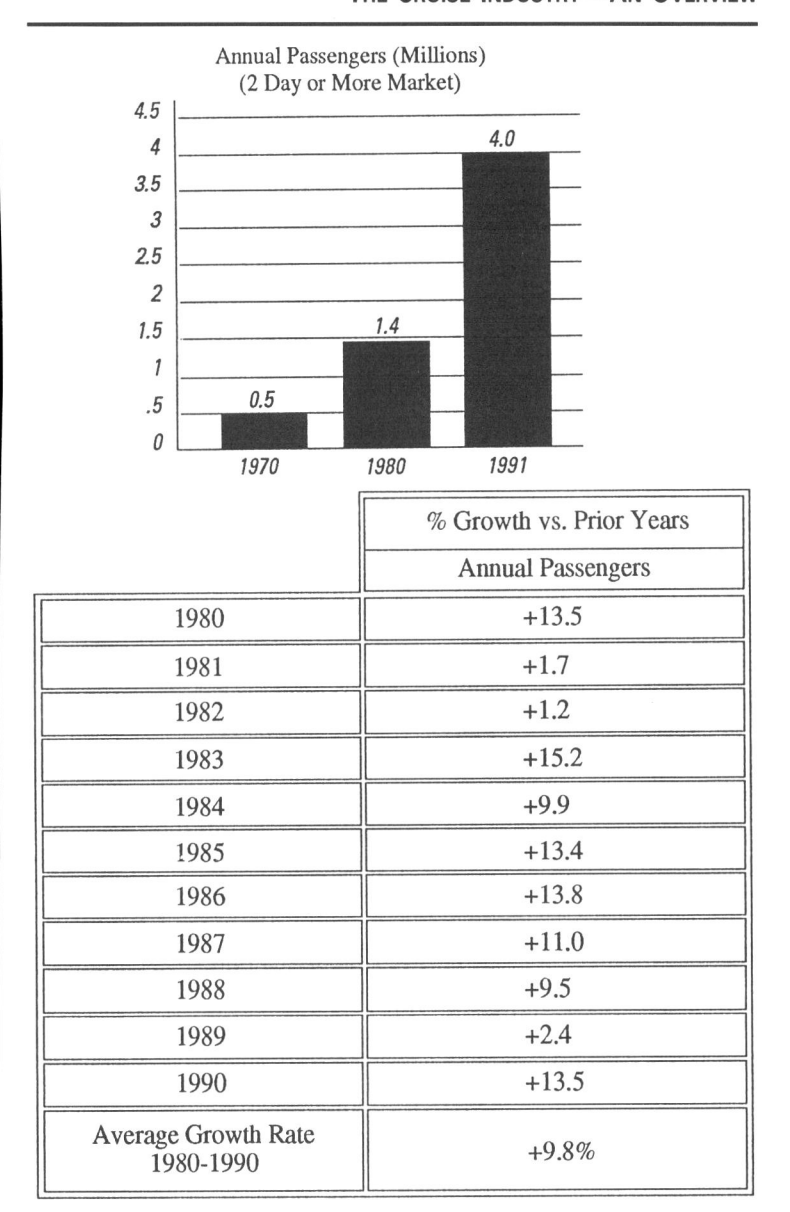

Annual Passengers (Millions)
(2 Day or More Market)

- 1970: 0.5
- 1980: 1.4
- 1991: 4.0

	% Growth vs. Prior Years Annual Passengers
1980	+13.5
1981	+1.7
1982	+1.2
1983	+15.2
1984	+9.9
1985	+13.4
1986	+13.8
1987	+11.0
1988	+9.5
1989	+2.4
1990	+13.5
Average Growth Rate 1980-1990	+9.8%

The extraordinary growth rate of the cruise industry since 1970—almost 10 percent annually.

- ships, the dancers and entertainers may change costumes as many as twenty times an hour.
- Cruise ships are not decorated shabbily or haphazardly. Some boast contemporary, museum-class art worth millions of dollars.
- The five most popular cruise ports and those from which the most people sail are Miami, Florida; San Juan, Puerto Rico; Port Everglades and Port Canaveral, Florida; and Los Angeles, California.
- The cruise lines with the most ships are Princess and Carnival (9 ships); Royal Caribbean, Epirotiki, and Renaissance (8 ships); Cunard (7 ships); Norwegian, Costa, and Chandris (6 ships); and Holland America (4 ships).
- The top five cruise destinations, those to which the most people sail, are the Caribbean Sea, the west coast of Mexico; Alaska; the Mediterranean Sea, and TransCanal (Panama).
- A total of thirty-six new ships are scheduled before 1995.

Trends in the Industry

Not only does the cruise industry continue to grow, but it continues to change in response to changing customer demographics, tastes, and interests. This has led to several noticeable trends in the 1990s, all of which have served to increase the alternatives available for people seeking the perfect vacation. Among the major trends are the following:

More educational cruises. People are taking cruises for more than just a relaxing vacation. Many want to make their time away from home not only enjoyable, but also educational. A number of cruise lines have met this interest with programs focusing on world affairs, botany, native lands and cultures, and computers. Many small ships, in particular, visit off-the-beaten-path ports and give passengers a much closer look and better understanding of the locale through lectures and field trips.

Theme cruises. In an effort to attract groups of people with a common interest, a number of lines have come up with innovative themes for cruises ranging from music to food. Those who enjoy big band music or tunes from the '50s and '60s have several choices for cruises devoted to those themes. People wanting a taste of mystery and suspense can take a murder-mystery cruise. Sports enthusiasts might schedule their trip on a special sports cruise where they'll have the opportunity to meet stars of football, basketball, or baseball. A number of lines also design an entire cruise around the destinations they visit—Delta Queen, for instance, with its nonstop dixieland jazz and bluegrass music, and American Hawaii, with classes on lei making, the Hawaiian language, and playing the ukulele.

More sports and fitness facilities. Gone are the days when a walk on deck was the only form of exercise available on a cruise ship. Those same ships now offer state-of-the-art programs and facilities that rival those of the top health clubs and spas. Most ships offer aerobics classes for every age from young to old. Larger ships offer volleyball and basketball on deck. Inside, exercise and weight rooms are filled with machines so that passengers don't have to break their routine of stepping or cycling. For those interested in less strenuous fitness activities, new European-style spas such as those on NCL's *Norway* and Costa's *CostaClassica* provide whirlpools, massages, and facial therapies.

More families are cruising. The kids are not being left at home anymore while Mom and Dad take a cruise. The kids are going along for the ride, and the cruise lines provide people and programs to keep them entertained from embarkation to debarkation. Premier Cruise Lines, the official cruise line of Walt Disney World, has Mickey Mouse, Donald Duck, and Goofy as part of its crew. Other ships are staffed with youth coordinators who take the kids on special tours and organize competitive games and "Coketail" parties. Newer ships also have video game rooms and large screen TVs complete with VCRs.

More places to visit. As the number of cruise lines increases, the number of itineraries is increasing as well. More ships are visiting Alaska during the summer months. The southern Caribbean is also being visited more often, as people tire of the same old ports in the eastern and western Caribbean. Hawaii is becoming more popular as people seek a new way to experience the islands. Smaller ships, especially, are leading the way to new ports because of their ability to sail into places the larger ships can't. Whether it be up the Amazon River or around the coast of Africa, people wanting to enjoy a more intimate atmosphere and to see something different are finding exotic new itineraries.

The ships are getting smaller—and bigger! The past three years have seen an influx of new lines and ships offering passengers a less crowded, more yacht-like, cruise experience. *Sea Goddess, Renaissance,* and several others have introduced a new way to cruise, far removed from the hustle and bustle and all-day organized activities of the superliners. These ships offer few if any organized activities. Passengers are free to do what they want when they want, and their cabins are likely to have a TV and VCR and a full-size bath.

But ships are also getting larger. Those lines catering to the middle-income level have brought out megaliners capable of carrying over 2,000 passengers. These ships, which could hold several of the "yachts," offer

The Cruise Industry—An Overview

(Top left) A sports platform unfolds from the stern of the Club Med 1. *(Top right) The revolutionary SSC* Radisson Diamond, *with twin-hull design. (Bottom left) The* Wind Spirit *and* Wind Star *of Windstar Cruises represent luxury sail cruising at its best. (Bottom right) Premier Cruise Lines is the official line of Walt Disney World.*

passengers any number of things to do, while increasing the owners' revenue and profits.

More ships offer a true "sailing" experience. Windjammer Cruises has always offered its Barefoot Cruises, but new lines now offer the same experience but with a higher-tech, higher-comfort touch. Windstar was the first to introduce computer-controlled, luxury sailing ships. Cruisers enjoy all the benefits of the smaller ships beneath four wind-powered, machine-controlled sails. Club Med has also sought to capture the excitement of this type of cruising with its new ships, the *Club Med I* and *II*.

The average cruise length is shorter. Following the demographic trend that has left individuals, couples, and families with less and less free time, the cruise lines have introduced several new ships to serve the growing three- and four-day cruise market. In the past, many of the passengers on these cruises were first-time cruisers or the very budget-oriented. Now the deciding factor may have nothing to do with finances, but simply the fact that a person can get away from work only for a long weekend.

The average age of passengers is younger. Cruising is no longer exclusively a vacation choice for the retired and wealthy. Many ships and lines continue to cater to this crowd, but many more lines offer cruising as an alternative to those younger and with less money to spend on a vacation. As the number of ships has increased and images of cruising have been sent into millions of homes via TV, the market has widened to include more of these twenty-five to forty-year-olds. They are coming aboard as singles, as newlyweds, and as families with their young children. The net effect is that in the past two years the number of passengers ages twenty-five to forty has increased by a third.

More of "the ultimate in luxury." New lines (Majesty, Crystal, Seabourn, and others), new divisions of existing lines (Chandris's Celebrity Cruises), and new individual ships (Royal Viking's all-suite *Queen*) present first-time and repeat cruisers with many more choices without having to compromise their standards. More spacious cabins, better views of the sea, and tens of millions worth of decorative furnishings make cruising on these ships a first-class experience.

The big lines keep getting bigger. The past few years have seen a consolidation in the cruise industry similar to that in the airline industry. Carnival consumed Holland America and Windstar, Royal Caribbean merged with Admiral, and Princess converted Sitmar. This has left fewer lines with much larger fleets and dominance in the industry. Five companies (Carnival, Kloster, P and O, Royal Caribbean, and Cunard) now control almost half the ships in the membership of the Cruise Line International Association.

THE ROLE OF THE TRAVEL AGENT

It is estimated that 95 to 97 percent of cruises are booked through travel agents. Why? Because of the valuable middleman role that agents play in the marketing, selling, and arranging of cruise vacations.

First, agencies help the cruise lines promote awareness of cruising as a vacation option. Through cooperative agreements with a line, an agency may participate in a newspaper advertisement in the Sunday travel section or may put on an event such as a cruise night. The agency advertises the cruise night to its customers, giving them an opportunity to enjoy food, drink, and maybe entertainment while visiting displays of a number of cruise lines. Promotional gifts and door prizes generate additional interest.

Once someone is interested in taking a cruise, the travel agent assumes the important role of advisor and consultant. A week-long cruise for two or more people is an expensive investment. Many factors must be considered when choosing which cruise to take, and an experienced travel agent is the one to make the customer aware of all the options.

The factors that are important in matching a person with the right cruise include the following:

- **The average age of the passengers.** A couple of twenty-five-year-olds wanting to party and have fun won't have too much of it on a ship that caters to the over-fifty-five crowd. Conversely,

a group of senior citizens may be terrorized on a cruise with a group of recent high school graduates. It is the agent's job to make sure clients go on cruises designed for their age groups.
- **Size of the ship**. There's something to be said for both large and small ships. Large ships offer much larger facilities and sometimes many more entertainment options. The drawback, of course, is that there are also many more people on board. Smaller ships offer a more relaxed environment and usually the opportunity to get to know other passengers and the crew much better. The client's choice between activities and solitude plays a large part in which cruise a travel agent recommends.
- **Personal taste**. Someone who hates Italian food may not eat much on one of the many cruise ships that are Italian-registered and -oriented. "Taste" applies not only to food but also to activities. People seeking a cruise to relax and do things at their own pace may not react too well to the organized activities and meal schedules found on most larger ships. They would be much better suited to one of the smaller ships that offer open seating for meals and few planned activities.
- **Budget or money available**. Of course, price is a major factor in choosing a cruise. A recent college graduate or young professional probably cannot afford a twelve-day cruise to Alaska, but a four-day cruise to the Bahamas may be perfect. More affluent adults or families may find that they can manage a much nicer vacation than they expected, depending on what is available. Here is where travel agents perform one of their most valuable functions. Pointing out discounts, specials, or reduced fares, they may be able to

save a couple or a family several hundred dollars on the cost of their cruise vacation.
- **Cabin arrangements**. Cabins and their sizes are discussed in detail elsewhere in the book. But it is particularly applicable here because first-time cruisers may not be aware of the space limitations in the typical cabin. They may decide that rather than choosing the cheapest fare and being crammed in with several other people, they would rather pay more and have only two in the cabin or get a larger cabin or a suite.
- **Itinerary**. Although it's easy enough to look through a brochure and see where a ship goes, a travel agent can tell vacationers which cruise going to which ports offers the best shopping, watersports, or whatever other activities they are interested in. Agents can also provide valuable advice on what types of identification, special shots, or currency might be needed in those locales.

	Percent of Revenue Generated Through Travel Agents
Cruises	95% +
Airlines	70-80%
Hotels	10-20%
Car Rentals	20-60%

Travel agents provide a valuable service both to vacationers and the cruise lines.

- **Climate.** Not all people would enjoy a vacation in the scorching heat of the Caribbean. Those who prefer milder temperatures might prefer a cruise up the Mississippi River or to New England or Canada. For even cooler temperatures, there are summer cruises to Alaska. And for those who would rather wear a parka and gloves than a bathing suit, there are educational and adventure cruises to Antarctica. A travel agent knows the typical climate to be found in most ports around the world and can send clients where they will be most comfortable.

A good agent is aware of the importance of all these factors and knows which lines offer each. The agents' advice and hand-holding until the departure date make them a valuable resource for consumers. The service they provide in booking clients makes them valuable to the cruise lines. Thus, their role is vital in the chain of events from helping people choose a ship to actually getting them on it.

THE ROLE OF THE CLIA

The Cruise Lines International Association (CLIA) has the largest membership of cruise lines in the world as well as the largest number of travel agency affiliates in North America. Currently, thirty-two cruise lines carrying 97 percent of North American-generated passengers belong to the CLIA. More than 20,000 travel agents are affiliated.

The association, based in New York City, is run by a staff presided over by a chairman and vice chairman from the member cruise lines. The CLIA's main goals are to promote its member lines to travel agencies and the public and to provide training and tools to assist travel agency affiliates in selling cruises.

The Cruise Industry—An Overview

The CLIA plays a valuable role in the industry by uniting cruise lines and agencies into one organization with a common purpose, and by supporting the growth of the industry through its marketing campaigns and the training and resources provided to those businesses selling cruises to the public. Its address is 500 Fifth Avenue, New York, NY 10110.

Encouter with a Hurricane

Tropical storms and hurricanes are quite frequent in the Caribbean, but they rarely affect cruises. Because they take several days to form, their probable course can be charted, allowing most ships to change their itinerary and avoid them. Occasionally one cannot be avoided, and passengers are forced off once sunny decks and inside the ship. Rarely, however, is a ship caught directly in the path of a hurricane.

In 1988 I found myself in the middle of one of those "rare" situations. The crew and the passengers were made aware that on our cruise to the island of Barbados we would cross paths with a hurricane slowly brewing in the area. Since there was nothing to do but hope for the best, the crew declared a "Hurricane Party" to help take minds off the imminent danger.

The night before we were due at Barbados, the ship rolled in choppy seas and heavy rain. Down in the crew cabins, those not scheduled to work partied with an assortment of Caribbean beverages and food, oblivious of the weather. We had contests for the gaudiest outfits and for who could stuff the most cheesepuffs in their mouths, and we came up with our own cast of "The Love Boat" complete with reputation-damaging nicknames.

The next day we sailed into Barbados as planned. The weather was only overcast so the passengers were allowed to go into port as scheduled. Soon after lunch, however, the weather took a turn for the worse. The hurricane had changed direction and was moving closer to the island. To avoid being tossed against the concrete docks, the ship would have to put out to sea.

When this announcement was made over the intercom, panic struck among the passengers. All those aboard at the time had husbands, wives, and other family members who were ashore. What would happen to them? Were we going to leave them on the island to face the hurricane? The answer was yes. Official personnel would stay in the terminal area to gather them as they returned, but the ship would have to put to sea to avoid severe damage at the pier.

A table was set up in the main showroom, and all passengers and crew reported to it so that pursers could account for those not on the ship. Just before the ship was ready to cast off, however, good news came. The hurricane would not come close enough to require the ship to leave port. Not only that, but instead of sailing at the scheduled time of just after dark, the captain decided to let us stay until midnight. We had an unexpected good time enjoying the open-air restaurants and abundant nightlife of downtown Barbados.

Don Kennedy

3

The Job Market

Any job that offers free living quarters, all the food you can eat, and free travel to some of the most beautiful places on earth is going to appeal to a lot of people. Working on a cruise ship offers all of those benefits and does attract a lot of candidates. Cruise line personnel offices are swamped with applications from all over the world. Most of these applicants are not seriously interested in a career on cruise ships; they just want to enjoy the sun and fun for a while. Many have no special education or experience that qualifies them to work on a ship; they just apply to see what kind of response they get. When they don't get one at all, they usually quit trying.

How to Beat the Competition
The way to get yourself noticed and to get a job on a ship is to be what those people are not—serious, qualified, and persistent. These three qualities are discussed in detail in later chapters: being qualified in Chapter 4, being persistent in Chapter 8, and being seriously committed in Chapter 12. If you already consider yourself to have all three qualities and you follow the strategies outlined in this book, you still can't be guaranteed a job, but your chances will be greatly increased.

WHY SO MANY JOBS ARE AVAILABLE

You may be wondering, "If the jobs are so great, why are there any available?" It is reasonable to assume that once people get a taste of the good life working on a ship, they would never want to leave. But that is not the case. People do leave for a number of reasons, and in the process, they create vacancies for others looking for their first job on board.

First, crew members take vacations and people must be hired to fill their positions while they are gone. Crew members may work six months on, one month off, or one year on, two months off. If you can get hired to fill in for a vacationing crew member, it is likely that you'll be asked to stay permanently, possibly on another ship, once (or if) the person you replaced returns.

Second, crew members get other jobs. Just as on land, if a person is offered a better job somewhere else, he'll leave his current one. Many crew members are able to parlay the people experience they gain working on a cruise ship into an even better position on land.

Third, and ironically, that same exposure to people is another reason many leave. When you live and work on a cruise ship, you are "trapped" in a confined environment with up to a couple of thousand demanding people. Passengers have paid a lot of money for their cruise, and they expect a lot. Because you wear a uniform, you are easily identified as a crew member and are a favorite target of criticism, complaints, and requests. The inability to "get away from it all," like going home and putting your feet up after a hard day at work, burns many people out. They decide to go back to a land job so that where they "live" and where they "work" are not the same.

Fourth, many crew members leave simply because they miss home. Being away from your friends and family for several months in a row can be trying,

New megaliners hold from 1,500 to 2,500 passengers. (Top) **Regal Princess**; *(bottom)* **Crown Princess.**

especially if you've never done it before. Some cruise lines have special programs permitting crew members to bring their families aboard once a year. But many people are uncomfortable with several months of separation and eventually decide to return to a more stable life-style.

Fifth, and last, are the normal reasons of promotion or termination. When a crew member is moved up or fired, a position is left to be filled. Because of the turnover caused by the first four reasons, promotions can occur rapidly for those who stay; it may be possible to reach Cruise Director in as little as four years. Each time a person does move up, someone is hired to fill the position. Very few people are fired on ships, but it does happen for receiving several passenger complaints, for use of drugs, or for missing the ship in port. Such dismissals create immediate job openings for applicants who join a ship on short notice.

Of course, not all the jobs become available because people leave. The stream of bigger and better ships going into service each year creates thousands of new jobs. As the cruise industry continues to grow, the need for qualified employees will grow, too. There's no question that the opportunity is there. Now you must evaluate whether you are qualified to pursue it.

A Typical Day as a Purser

As an assistant purser, I worked with the other members of the purser's staff in handling many of the administrative and financial operations of the ship. The Purser's Desk is much like the front desk of a hotel. It is where people come when they have a complaint about their luggage being lost or their room not having a double bed, or when they need to exchange money or lock up valuables for safekeeping.

Typically I worked only six hours a day, but that was almost always seven days a week. The other assistant purser and I were free to make our own schedules. If she wanted off in St. Thomas one week, I would take off in Barbados. If she wanted to go on a catamaran cruise in Martinique, I would work so that I could climb the waterfalls when the ship docked in Jamaica.

The shifts when the ship was in port were the easiest. Almost all the passengers would be ashore, so there was little to do. I usually kept a book at the desk to pass the time until a passenger came in need of something. The few hours before reaching port were not so easy. Everyone was rushing to cash travelers checks or exchange foreign currency. Our cash drawers held several thousand dollars, and responsibility in such an intense environment was essential. If you've worked in a bank during lunch time on Friday or in a hotel during morning checkout, you'll know what I mean.

The first few hours after the ship left home port in Miami were also tense. People who were dissatisfied with their room or dinner sitting or who had lost their luggage arrived for assistance. Handling these situations requires tolerance and patience. After paying several thousand dollars, people get upset when things don't turn out as expected. If you can deal with these passengers in an understanding way, you can manage any customer service situation you encounter in a job ashore.

Foreign language ability is an excellent skill to have as a purser. In fact, many cruise lines require it. I encountered countless situations where knowledge of Spanish or French would have been an asset. One of a purser's duties is handling customs and immigration paperwork for employees and passengers. Many of them speak little or no English, and your ability to help will make you an indispensable part of the staff.

Pursers wear uniforms because they are considered officers. The uniforms are typically provided by the line the day before you board the ship. The dress whites can be a source of pride as you walk about the ship, but they can also be a pain because they make you a magnet for anyone with a problem or a complaint.

As a purser, I ate in the officers' mess. We had a nice dining room, great food, and two waiters to serve us. News releases were on the tables so that we could keep up with what was going on in the world, and a TV set played whatever was on the ship's channel.

The Purser's Desk closed early, leaving us with plenty of time after dinner to do whatever we wanted. When you first board a ship, you want to see every show. But once you've done that, you're much more likely to attend parties being held in various cabins or just retire to read or listen to music.

A "typical" day depends on when you work and whether you're in port or at sea. The hours are not as long as some, but the job can be equally stressful with the number of passengers who come to you to solve problems. It's fun to enjoy the privileges accorded you as an officer, but it's important to remember that you are at the bottom of the chain of command.

Don Kennedy

4

What It Takes—Qualifications and Skills

THE BASIC REQUIREMENTS
There are very few absolute requirements to be met for every cruise line. Each has its own policies and procedures for hiring and promotion. One fact you can count on, however, is that their requirements and the backgrounds of their crew members will be diverse.

The standard requirements, or the areas in which all lines have some established goals, are listed below. Satisfying these is the first hurdle in your campaign.

Health
As cruise ships have only minor medical facilities on board, they are unequipped to treat an ongoing or long-term medical condition. Therefore, all crew candidates must pass a standard physical to assure that they have no major medical problems that might interfere with performance of their job.

Age
It is unlikely that you will be hired until you're at least eighteen years of age. Most of the crew are twenty-five to forty-five, except for some of the higher-ranking officers, who may be older. All are enthusiastic and

outgoing, however, and it can be very beneficial to learn to socialize with age groups other your own.

Education

As in many jobs, an education in a related field may not be necessary, but it certainly won't hurt. Some crew members have college degrees, but many do not. Some went to trade schools to learn what they do on the ship—anything from hairstyling to casino dealing to massage; others learned it on the job. As is reasonable to expect, the more education you have in the area for which you are applying, the better your chances of being hired. Take every opportunity to learn a skill valuable to the lines (listed in the next section), but remember that lack of school training can be compensated for by other factors.

Experience

Some jobs, such as beautician or bartender, require previous experience. You don't learn to cut hair on people who go to expensive salons at home. In fact, most cruise lines want you to have some kind of experience regardless of what position you are applying for. But some employees without work experience are hired and trained in the job on board. These jobs typically are in the food and beverage department, the hotel department, and occasionally the retail shops or casinos.

Foreign Languages

If you know one or more foreign languages, it will help you, no matter which line you apply to for a job. In two situations knowing another language may even be required: first, to work on a ship that sails to ports around the world, and second, to work for an upscale

WHAT IT TAKES—QUALIFICATIONS AND SKILLS

MARTINIQUE

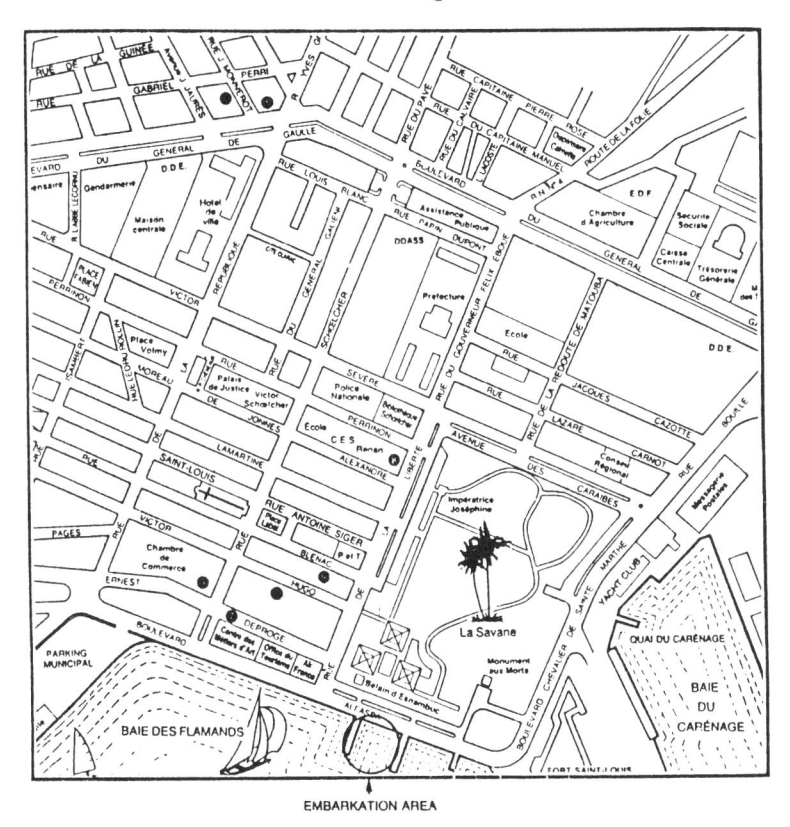

Foreign languages are important in a port such as Martinique, where French is spoken exclusively. A map of downtown Fort-de-France around the cruise ship docking area.

line that caters to an international clientele. In both situations, you must be able to communicate with passengers in their own language to serve them effectively. Language usually is not a problem, however, on

American-flag ships or those that sail exclusively in the Caribbean, as most of the passengers will be American.

Personality
The one requirement for every job on every line is an outgoing personality. On a cruise ship you serve people, period. The passengers expect to be pampered and entertained, and every crew member plays a part in fulfilling that expectation. You must love people—greeting them, meeting them, and creating an unforgettable vacation for them. Even with years of experience, a college degree, and the ability to speak four languages, if you never smile or if you are quick to anger, you won't last long.

KEY SKILLS

If you meet all the basic requirements, the next step is to decide what specific skills and experience you have that might interest the cruise lines. These are what you would highlight in your résumé (discussed in Chapter 7) and stress during phone conversations with personnel. The more you have to offer, the better your chances.

Because some cruise ships employ over 800 crew members performing a variety of tasks, it would be impractical to try to cover each job. Instead, the following is a list of skills, educational majors, and work areas that could be utilized in one or more groups of positions. The list is by no means all-inclusive. If you have an additional skill that might be of value, by all means include it in your application.

Foreign languages
Foreign travel
Travel and tourism

What It Takes—Qualifications and Skills

Hotel management
Hospitality management
Restaurant management
Cooking
Waiting tables
Bartending
Food and beverage services
Business administration
Office management
Banking
Management
Accounting
Entertainment
Music
Sound and light technology
Disc-jockeying
Physical fitness and education
Dance
Recreation and leisure services
Athletics
Teaching
Baby-sitting
Day-care center work
Camp counseling
Beauty care
Cosmetology
Manicuring
Massage
Fashion merchandising
Photography
Retail sales
Casino operations
Medicine
Engineering
Painting

The Neon Bar on Carnival Cruise Lines' **Ecstasy.** *An outgoing personality and love of people are necessary to entertain passengers seven days a week.*

Carpentry
Welding
Electrical work
Security
Cleaning/janitorial
Scuba
Water sports
Water safety
Computers
Cash handling
Military service
ROTC
Government work

What It Takes—Qualifications and Skills

Be sure not to disqualify yourself before the cruise lines do. You may have majored in botany or engineering in college, but if you have traveled abroad, have five years of watersports experience, and have a great personality, these will more than compensate for the unrelated major. It may be your work experience rather than of your schooling—or vice versa—that stands out on a résumé and gets you the job.

Your Personal Qualities

If you think you meet the basic requirements and have some of the work and education skills, your last step is to evaluate yourself on the personal qualities most successful crew members seem to have.

Luck. You'll need at least a little of this to be hired. As many qualified applications as the cruise lines receive, you need every extra edge possible. Getting your application in at just the right time, knowing someone who works for the lines, or living close to a line's home office may be all the break you need.

People skills. If you don't get along with people, you'll be getting off the ship fast (possibly involuntarily). Not only will you be serving and entertaining people of other races and religions, but you might even be bunking with them in the same crew cabin.

An adventurous spirit. The ships will take you to places you've never seen. There'll be opportunities to climb mountains and dive in seas. The unadventurous will feel left out as the other crew members and passengers rush to enjoy the excitement.

A love of travel. This goes hand in hand with the adventurous spirit. On a ship you'll go to sleep in one country and wake up in another. Those who enjoy travel will be enthralled.

A good attitude and a sense of humor. If you can make rough seas a fun event and turn passengers' problems into opportunities to serve, you've got the right attitude. Things happen throughout the day that irritate some people, but challenge others. A good attitude will not only make you well liked by the crew, but also a favorite of the passengers.

Ability to handle stress. Dealing with passengers who have paid several thousand dollars for a vacation and expect to get their money's worth can be stress-inducing. It obviously goes with the territory. How you handle angry passengers, an unexpectedly long line, and other such situations will determine whether you enjoy your job or burn out after six months.

Public-speaking ability. Whether you're a cruise staff member doing a comic routine, or a waiter presenting the night's dessert choices, speaking in front of six to six hundred people had better not disturb you. Regardless of your job, it's likely that at some point you'll have to get up in front of several passengers at once.

Genuine kindness and caring. Making sure the passengers enjoy the cruise they've always dreamed of is what it's all about. It's the little things like getting them an extra spoon, leaving a mint on their pillow, or helping them off the tender and up the gangway that demonstrate

What It Takes—Qualifications and Skills

your empathy and insure that they have the best cruise possible.

Good grooming. Cruise ships don't hire unattractive people. Long, unkempt hair, poor personal hygiene, or shabby clothes will guarantee that you don't get hired. Keep your body clean and your appearance neat.

Patience. If you expect to be hired immediately after sending in your application, you will probably be disappointed. It takes an extremely well-connected, qualified, or lucky applicant to be hired quickly. It is much more likely to take two to four weeks for your résumé to be reviewed and then another two to four if you are lucky enough to receive an application and you return it promptly. You have to be patient waiting to hear from a cruise line; but once you do, you'll probably need the next quality.

Ability to leave on short notice. This is discussed later in the book, but it is relevant to mention here because it is one of those unwritten qualifications that may be essential to your being hired. If you're lucky, you'll get several weeks' notice, but it is much more likely that you'll get less than a week's. If you can leave that soon (which can be difficult if you are in an apartment lease or have children), you'll get the job. If you can't, someone else will.

Flexibility. You must be flexible as to hours of work. A ship operates twenty-four hours a day, and your job may require you to open the disco at 10 p.m. (disc jockey) or to open the coffee and croissant buffet at sunrise (cook/server/waiter). If you are enamored of the nine-to-five routine, you won't be happy with most cruise ship jobs.

Ability to handle lack of privacy. On a cruise ship, your "work" place is your "home" place. You can't get away from it. You don't have a cozy little house in the suburbs (you'll probably be sharing a windowless cabin), and you don't have a private yard (but you can lie on deck with 500 to 1,500 other people). There is little chance to get away from people, as even the ports you visit are usually crowded with tourists. Expect to be deprived of privacy while you're on board, and make up for it when you go on vacation.

The capacity to save money. A frequent question about working on a cruise ship is, "How much can I make?" That's not the important question. The correct one is, "How much can I save?" You can put away some serious money, even in an entry-level job, if you have the capacity to save money. There's much temptation to spend it—drinks on the ship, food in port, and clothes and souvenirs from both. Do have fun, but resist the urge to do everything. Remember you're not on vacation, you're working. If you don't put away something each month, you'll get off the ship at the end of your contract with nothing but memories.

Commitment and persistence. This is discussed elsewhere in the book, so I'll mention it only briefly here. The main message is that if you give up after one rejection or even fifteen, you'll never get the job. If you believe you are qualified and are not just applying on a whim, you

WHAT IT TAKES—QUALIFICATIONS AND SKILLS

must be committed to sending as many applications as it takes and persisting until you finally get the job you desire.

How I Got My Job as a Teen Counselor
I went on my first cruise with my family during Christmas in 1986. I was a junior in college and majoring in Leisure Studies. Once I stepped aboard M/S *Song of America*, it didn't take me long to decide that I wanted to be a part of my own cruise ship family.

During the days at sea, my brother Michael and I would lie on deck and listen to the steel band. We would watch the crew members try to recruit passengers for various pool games. One of the staff members looked familiar to both Michael and me. After talking with her, we realized that we all worked for the same beach service in the summers. She was now working as a youth counselor during the Christmas holidays. I asked her how I could get such a job for next Christmas. She gave me the name of the personnel director at Royal Caribbean Cruise Line, and suggested that I write to her and tell her how much I wanted to work for the line.

After our cruise, I followed her advice and wrote to the company. While I was in my senior year, the cruise line informed me that I had the job as youth counselor on the M/S *Sun Viking* for the upcoming two-week Christmas cruise.

The cruise line offered me the same job after I graduated—this time for June, July, and August, on the same ship.

During my time as a teen counselor, coordinating games and activities for teens twelve to seventeen, I got to visit all the Caribbean islands and to meet many interesting people. I could not believe that I was getting paid for having so much fun!

Suzanne Kelley

5

Positions Available

If you have passed the test and come to the conclusion that you are right for the cruise industry, now you must decide which job is right for you. Many people who apply for work with a cruise line are so eager to be hired that they state their willingness to do "anything" just to get on board. This failure to specify a position can be one of the biggest mistakes an applicant can make. You are basically saying that you have no outstanding job skills and that you're not sure how you could help the cruise line; you just want to work on one of their ships.

Such hopeful pleading won't move your application into the "next to be hired" stack. To stand out, you must know what position you want, how you are qualified for it, and why you are the best candidate to fill it. To know all that, you must have a general idea of what the various crew members on a cruise ship do.

THE TYPICAL STAFF STRUCTURE
First, you should be aware of the way most crews are structured—that is, the groups in which positions are categorized. There are basically three: officers; cruise staff; and hotel, food and beverage, and deck and engine staff.

Officers

As you might expect, the officers of the ship are the highest-ranking members of the crew. They wear uniforms similar to those worn by U.S. Navy officers. They live in officers' cabins, sometimes on their own deck, near the top of the ship. They have meals in an officers' dining room or, on some ships, with the passengers in the main dining room. In either case, they usually get to enjoy the same great food the passengers do.

Before you set your sights too high, however, there is one other consideration. Officers on most ships are not American. They are Greek, Norwegian, or Italian and have graduated from their country's marine academy or served in its merchant marine, or both. It is very difficult, if not impossible, for an American to reach officer's rank in the operations division. The exceptions are the purser and the food and beverage departments, where it may be possible, even at entry-level, to achieve officer status.

Also, on the cruise lines that operate only from and to U.S. ports—American Hawaii and Delta Queen, for example—only Americans are hired. All positions, from officer down to busboy, are filled by Americans. If you have thought of joining the Navy or merchant marine but don't want to make a career of it, becoming an officer on one of these American cruise lines may be the perfect job for you.

Cruise Staff

The cruise staff comprises the greatest variety of positions, but all have essentially the same mission: to serve and entertain the passengers. The positions included in this category vary from ship to ship, but like the officers, they generally share the same privileges and live and eat together on the ship.

The core of the cruise staff are those whose main responsibility is arranging and hosting activities for the passengers. They create and manage the multitude of games, contests, and shows that occur on a typical cruise. Since a large part of their work is socializing with the passengers, these crew members are generally free to go anywhere on the ship and to dance, sunbathe, and go on tours just like the passengers. Both men and women fill these positions. Having an additional talent such as singing or dancing can improve your chances of being hired, since the cruise staff participate in many of the shows.

Many types of entertainers and entertainment are provided on a ship. All ships offer musical entertainment ranging from cocktail pianist to reggae band to full pops orchestra. The size and type of music groups depend on the ship's itinerary and size, and the average age of its passengers. Most larger ships also employ dance troupes who perform Broadway-style shows in the main showroom each night. Usually a sound and light technician operates the equipment for these shows as well as assisting the DJ who provides music for dancing in the disco.

Most lines have visiting entertainers who travel from ship to ship serving as headliners for the shows. These entertainers usually have years of experience and may work for several cruise lines at one time. If you think you're qualified for one of these positions, plan on submitting at least one audio and video tape of your act.

Some staff members provide activities for the children on board so that the parents are free to take tours, attend shows, or just have time alone. The job is a cross between baby-sitting and running a day-care center. On some ships it is not a paying position but gives you the opportunity to live on a cruise ship for the summer in exchange for working with the kids a few hours each day.

The recreation and fitness staff operate those facilities, which range from full-size European spas to on-deck aerobic workouts. Good health and some athletic education or experience are essential for this job.

The beauty salon offers everything from hairstyling to manicures and, on some ships, therapeutic massages. If you already work in a beauty salon or one of these other areas, you have all the experience necessary for a position on a cruise ship.

The retail staff work in the duty-free shops and stores found on most ships. On smaller vessels, this may be only a large gift shop. But newer, larger ships may have stores selling everything from flipflops to furs. An advantage of being part of this staff is that by law the stores must be closed while the ship is in port, so as not to compete with the city's merchants. Unless they're doing inventory, the retail staff is free to go ashore in every port.

Other staff members who usually have privileges comparable to those of the cruise staff are the photographers and those who work in the casino. All rank somewhere below the officers and above the rest of the crew. Their cabins, like their rank, are usually between those of the officers at the top of the ship and the other crew members at the bottom. They eat in cruise staff dining rooms or, on many ships, with the passengers in the main dining room.

Most cruise staff members are free to use all areas of the ship, but some ships do restrict access to public rooms. As a cruise staff member, you can often feel more like a passenger than an employee. And, unlike the officers' positions, almost all of these are open to Americans. As the crew members most responsible for entertainment they must speak the language and share the values of the passengers, the majority of whom are Americans.

HOTEL, FOOD AND BEVERAGE, AND DECK AND ENGINE STAFF

Last in the hierarchy of rank and privileges, but certainly not in importance, are the hotel, food and beverage, and deck and engine staffs. These three groups have very distinct functions. The hotel staff clean and service passenger rooms and all public areas. The food and beverage staff serve food and drink in the many dining rooms, cafes, showrooms, and bars all over the ship. The deck and engine crew perform all duties related to the mechanical operation and physical maintenance of the ship.

Each of these departments has a rank structure from officer to entry-level. The officers, of course, enjoy the privileges and benefits discussed earlier. It is the average member of these staffs, however—about two thirds of the crew—that works the hardest and longest without enjoying the privileges of the officers or cruise staff. Room stewards and waiters, for example, serve passengers off and on from morning until midnight. When they are not working, they are not free to mingle with the passengers in the public areas.

The other side of the story, however, is that these crew members can make substantial money. Because their pay comes almost entirely from tips, they can make a lot of money by providing unmatched personal service to passengers. It might be worth trading some of the fun for the extra income if your goal is to work for a while to save money.

The deck and engine crew are discussed only briefly here. People don't dream of working on a ship so that they can work at the bottom of the ship fixing it or hanging from the side in 100-degree Caribbean sun painting it. Furthermore, like the operations officers, most of

EXPLORING CAREERS ON CRUISE SHIPS

Food and Beverage staff members serve passengers in the dining room, in bars, in cabins, and on deck.

these positions are available only to Greek, Italian, or Norwegian seamen. And even they are facing reduced opportunities, as many lines are utilizing cheaper labor hired in the Philippines.

ON BOARD POSITIONS
This section is structured to give you the basic information necessary to decide what job is right for you. Read

through all of them, and then decide which best suits you and your interests. That should be the specific position you apply for.

Cruise Director/Assistant Cruise Director
Duties: Organize, schedule, and direct activities and programs.
Supervise cruise staff, bands, and entertainment.
Pay: $3,000 to $5,000 per month plus bonus.

Cruise Staff Members
Duties: Host organized activities.
Socialize at shows, parties, embarkation, and debarkation.
Pay: $1,500 to $2,500 per month.

Hostess
Duties: Represent Captain at social functions.
Assist with other cruise staff activities.
Pay: $1,600 to $2,600 per month.

Shore Excursion Director
Duties: Provide information and sell tickets for tours.
Liaison with tour companies in port of call.
Pay: $1,900 to $2,400 per month.

Recreation/Fitness Director
Duties: Organize and operate fitness programs.
Assist with other cruise staff activities.
Pay: $1,400 to $1,900 per month.

Youth Coordinator
Duties: Organize and operate programs to entertain youth.

Assist with other cruise staff activities.
Pay: $900 to $1,400 per month.

Dancer
Duties: Entertain in nightly shows and revues.
May assist with other cruise staff duties such as teaching dancing or aerobics.
Pay: $1,200 to $1,700 per month.

Musician
Duties: Play at nightly shows and revues.
Play at welcome aboard and cocktail parties.
Pay: $1,600 to $2,100 per month.

Entertainer (ship to ship)
Duties: Main act at nightly shows and revues.
May assist with other cruise staff activities.
Pay: $400 to $1,200 per week.

Disc Jockey
Duties: Play music in disco and at parties and events.
Assist with other cruise staff activities.
Pay: $1,400 to $1,900 per month.

Sound and Light Technician
Duties: Manage all sound and light equipment used for entertainment.
Run lighting and sound for nightly shows and revues.
Pay: $2,100 to $2,600 per month.

Beautician
Duties: Perform hairstyling, manicures, and other beauty treatments.
Pay: $350 to $550 per week (including tips).

Positions Available

Masseuse
Duties: Perform massages.
Pay: $375 to $575 per week (including tips).

Retail Sales
Duties: Work in retail shops and boutiques. May participate in fashion shows and assist with inventory.
Pay: $1,000 to $1,400 per month.

Retail Manager
Duties: Manage and operate all retail shops and boutiques. May organize fashion shows and supervise inventory.
Pay: $25,000 to $35,000 (Assistant Manager—includes base + commission).
$40,000 to $50,000 (Manager—includes base + commission).

Casino Manager
Duties: Supervise casino staff and operations.
Pay: $45,000 to $60,000 per year.

Casino Dealer/Cashier
Duties: Run cards and other gambling games such as roulette. Exchange chips and other winnings for cash.
Pay: $200 to $400 per week (Cashier).
$300 to $500 per week (Dealer).

Scuba Instructor
Duties: Operate diving/snorkeling programs. Teach scuba/snorkeling classes.
Pay: $1,000 to $2,000 per month.

Photographer
Duties: Take photographs of passengers at special occasions.
Develop all pictures and sell through gallery on board.
Pay: $350 to $550 per week.

Purser
Duties: Manage administrative paperwork and payroll. Handle customer complaints and problems dealing with lost luggage, cabin dissatisfaction, and customs and immigration.
Pay: $1,200 to $3,200 per month.

Doctor
Duties: Manage health facilities on board.
Handle medical emergencies during a cruise.
Pay: Varies from free cruises up to $50,000 per year, depending on cruise line.

Nurse
Duties: Assist doctor in performance of medical duties.
Pay: Varies from free cruises to $35,000 per year, depending on cruise line.

Hotel Manager
Duties: Supervise purser and cruise staffs.
Supervise hotel, food, and beverage operations.
Pay: $40,000 to $60,000 per year.

Chief Steward
Duties: Supervise steward staff.
Manage housekeeping operations.
Pay: $2,100 to $2,600 per month.

Positions Available

Room Steward
Duties: Clean and maintain passenger rooms.
Pay: $50 per month plus tips (substantial).

Steward/Cleaner
Duties: General housekeeping and cleaning of public areas.
Pay: $200 to $500 per month.

Food and Beverage Manager/Assistant Manager
Duties: Supervise all F&B operations. Coordinate restocking of food/bar supplies in port.
Pay: $35,000 to $50,000 per year.

Maître d'Hôtel
Duties: On-floor management of the dining room.
Pay: $800 to $7,000 per week.

Headwaiter
Duties: Supervise one section of the dining room.
Pay: $500 to $700 per week.

Waiter
Duties: Serve at all meals.
Pay: $300 to $500 per week.

Busboy
Duties: Assist waiter with meal service. Clear tables to prepare for next course.
Pay: $200 to $400 per week.

Bar Manager
Duties: Supervise all bar operations.
Pay: $30,000 to $40,000 per year.

Bar Waiter
Duties: Serve drinks in all areas of ship.
Pay: $250 to $500 per week.

Wine Steward
Duties: Serve wine at meals.
Pay: $250 to $450 per week.

Don't Miss the Ship!

We had a casino girl on the ship who was always doing crazy things. One day in Nassau, she missed the ship! As it put out to sea, a small motorboat, honking its horn and full of people waving their arms frantically, pulled up alongside. After several minutes they finally got the attention of the officers on the bridge.

Upon a quick look through the binoculars, they recognized the casino girl. They brought the ship to a complete standstill—not an easy task, since its massive engines don't stop on a dime.

Once the ship was finally stopped, a rope ladder was thrown down. If you've ever seen someone attempt to climb a rope ladder, you know it's not that easy. Slowly, she struggled to the top and was helped aboard. As she landed on the deck, everyone thought she would be a nervous wreck. Instead, she sighed and said in her heavy British accent, "That was a bloody exhausting climb, but for the day I had, it was well worth every minute of it."

Unfortunately, I never did find out what she had done.

Juliann Pugh

6
Who's Hiring?—Where To Apply

Where a cruise line's ships go is not important for your first job on board. You shouldn't limit yourself to lines that sail to places you've always wanted to visit. Apply to all of them, and be happy to go wherever the ship goes, whether it's the Bahamas or Alaska. Your main goal is to get on board a ship and get cruise experience. Once you've got that, you can afford to be more selective about where you'd really like to work.

Two factors determine in what geographic areas you may eventually get the chance to work. The first is your language ability. Working on most cruise ships that visit the Caribbean, Mexico, or Alaska will probably not require you to know a second language. That is not true, however, for ships sailing to Europe, the Mediterranean, or the Far East. The majority of the passengers you encounter on those cruises will not be American and may not speak English. For you to be able to help them at all, you must be able to communicate with them in their native language. That could be Spanish, German, French, or even Japanese, depending upon the part of the world you are sailing in.

The other factor that determines where you sail is how long you'll be working on the ship. If you're looking for a full-time job and have no definite plans for leaving, there are no limits to the ships you could work on. You could do short cruises to the Bahamas or three-month cruises around the world. If you're working only for the summer or during a semester off from school, you'll most likely only get a chance to sail somewhere close to the U.S., most likely the Caribbean. The cost of flying you to another country is not worth it to the cruise line for the short time you'll be on board.

If you're fortunate enough to get on a ship that changes its itinerary every few months, you may get to visit several areas of the world within a year. But if not, enjoy the places you do visit. If you're sailing the summer in Alaska, you may not be able to put on a swimsuit as you would in the Caribbean, but you'll accumulate a whole different set of wonderful memories.

For a list of the ports that cruise ships visit most frequently, see Appendix A, Cruise Ship Ports Around the World.

Also, don't dismiss applying to a line because of the average age of its clientele. While knowing this fact is good, using it as a reason not to apply is bad. You might prefer to work for Carnival, which caters to young singles and families; but if Princess, which caters to a slightly older clientele, offers you your first job, take it! Do a great job for them, and then use that as leverage to get the job you really want with Carnival.

USING THE DIRECTORY

Even if you are applying to all the cruise lines, it is still helpful to know something about each of them. Having an idea of how big a line is, the names of its ships, and where they go shows that you've done some research and know whom you're applying to.

In Chapter 5 I talked about the importance of applying for a specific job. That is the first way in which you can gain an edge in your application efforts. The second

Who's Hiring?—Where to Apply

is to apply to the right place. You must know that the right person knows who you are and is at least considering you for a position. Addressing your materials to a specific person or department is the surest way to do that.

For that information to be up-to-date, you need to call the home offices listed in the following pages and find out who currently does the hiring for the positions you're interested in. They may give you the name of the person or just a department such as Human Resources. This step is extremely important; there may be as many as five places at a line where you might send your application, depending on what job you're applying for.

One secret that few applicants know is that there are outside companies, called concessions, which hire for specific groups of positions for more than one cruise line. A beauty concession, for example, might hire beauticians and massage therapists for five major lines. This is great for you as an applicant. By applying to these companies, you are automatically considered for several cruise lines. At the end of the cruise line directory (pages 101–102) is a list of these concessions grouped by positions they hire for. The best procedure is to send one application to an appropriate concession and another to the cruise line.

CRUISE LINE DIRECTORY

American Hawaii Cruises
American Hawaii has the only two oceangoing American-flag cruise ships. The *Constitution* and the *Independence* sail on three-day, four-day, and seven-day cruises through the Hawaiian Islands. The line began in 1980 with one ship and added the second in 1982. Together they offer a unique way to see Maui, Oahu, Kauai, and the Big Island of Hawaii.

Celebration

THE "FUN SHIPS" WELCOME ABOARD
Cruise Director
Steve Cassel

CAPTAIN RENATO PIOVANO

SATURDAY, DAY 1
Sunset: 6:36 p.m.

THE MASTER OF THE VESSEL WISHES TO EXTEND A PERSONAL WELCOME TO ALL PASSENGERS, HOPING THAT THIS CRUISE WILL BE A LONG REMEMBERED VACATION FOR ALL. ONCE AGAIN, WELCOME ABOARD!

Luggage will be delivered to your room as soon as possible. If you find any baggage in your cabin that doesn't belong to you, please notify the Purser or your Cabin Steward as soon as possible.

Time	Activity	Location
12:30–6:00 p.m.	Sail & Sign Credit Desk Opens	Promenade Desk
12:30–4:00 p.m.	Dining Room Reservations Made	Islands in the Sky Lounge
12:30–3:30 p.m.	Massage Appointment taken by Our Masseuse	Promenade Deck
1:30–4:00 p.m.	Video Diary Available, Underwater Camera and Snorkel Rentals	Main Deck
1:30–4:00 p.m.	Complimentary snacks served!	Wheelhouse Bar & Grill
2:00–4:00 p.m.	Beauty Salon opens for appointments only	Admiral Deck
2:00–4:00 p.m.	Our Calypso Band plays for your entertainment	Lido Deck Poolside
2:00–4:00 p.m.	Advance Tour tickets on sale	Shore Tours, Main Deck
2:00–4:00 p.m.	Disco opens for your enjoyment with DJ John	Promenade Deck
3:00–3:30 p.m.	Spa & Sports Talk	Astoria Lounge
4:00 p.m.	ms Celebration Sails for San Juan, Puerto Rico	
IMPORTANT:	Fire & Lifeboat Drill — The convention of Safety of Life at Sea and the U.S. Coast Guard makes this a command performance for all passengers. The drill will be held approximately 30 minutes after sailing. Please listen for the announcement. Thank you for your cooperation.	
	After our Departure and Lifeboat Drill the Full Casino will open till 3:00 a.m. Featuring Dice Tables, Roulette, Blackjack, Wheel of Fortune, Slot Machines and Poker	Rainbow Club Casino
4:00–8:00 p.m.	Appointments for Massage	Beauty Salon, Admiral Deck
6:00 p.m.	Main Sitting Dinner *Please check the color of your Dining Room Seating Card: Vista Dining Room: Yellow for Main Seating Horizon Dining Room: Orange for Main Sitting	Vista & Horizon Dining Rooms
7:00–8:00 p.m.	Shore tours on sale	Main Deck Lobby Area
7:15–8:00 p.m.	Complimentary Rum Swizzle Get Together. This is the perfect time to start meeting your fellow shipmates. Also enjoy our live Dixieland Band	Promenade Deck.
7:30–8:00 p.m.	Junior Cruiser Orientation Meeting. Bring your parents and meet your counselors.	Galax-Z Disco
8:00 p.m.	Late Sitting Dinner *Please check the color of your Dining Room Seating Card: Vista Dining Room: Blue for Late Seating Horizon Dining Room: Green for Late Sitting	Vista & Horizon Dining Rooms Admiral Deck Forward Admiral Deck Aft
8:15–9:00 p.m.	Dance to the music of the "Celebration Orchestra"	Astoria Lounge
9:00 p.m.	JACKPOT BINGO — Join us and win some extra shopping cash. We play progressive bingo with jackpots reaching hundreds of dollars! Come early for a good seat to see the show that follows! Snowball Game $1500.00	Astoria Lounge
9:30 p.m.	"Singles Party"! Complimentary Rum Swizzles & Dancing, Fun & Games	Galax-Z Disco
9:30 p.m.–LATE	Enjoy music at the Trolley Bar	Promenade Deck
9:30 p.m.–LATE	Live Music for your Dancing pleasure	Endless Summer Lounge
9:30 p.m.–LATE	Live Music for Dancing into the Night	Islands in the Sky Lounge
10:00 p.m.–3:00 a.m.	Disco opens (16 years and under must be with parents)	Galax-Z Disco
10:30 p.m.	SHOWTIME IN THE ASTORIA LOUNGE — Introduction of Cruise Staff along with fun & games.	
MIDNIGHT–1:30 a.m.	Midnight Buffet is served	Horizon Dining Room
1:30–2:30 a.m.	Mini Buffet is served at the Trolley	Promenade Deck
	Coffee available 24 hours a day on Lido Deck	

DRESS FOR THIS EVENING: Casual (Sunday evening will be our first formal night)
Movie: "The Fabulous Baker Boys" 1:00, 3:30, 6:00, 8:30, 11:00, 1:30 and 4:00 a.m.

Welcome Aboard activities sheet for the Carnival Cruise Lines ship Celebration.

Who's Hiring?—Where to Apply

American Hawaii Cruises
550 Kearny Street
San Francisco, CA 94108
(415) 392-9400

Ship: *Independence*
Number of Crew: 320
Number of Passengers: 798
Destination: Hawaii*

Ship: *Constitution*
Number of Crew: 320
Number of Passengers: 798
Destination: Hawaii

Carnival Cruise Lines

With over twenty years of cruising experience, Carnival is the largest cruise line in the world. Since 1972 it has offered affordable vacations for people of all ages. It began with one ship, the *Mardi Gras* and others soon followed: *Carnivale* (1975), *Festivale* (1978), *Tropicale* (1982), *Holiday* (1985), *Jubilee* (1986), *Celebration* (1987), *Fantasy* (1990), and *Ecstasy* (1991). *Sensation* and *Fascination* come on line in 1993 and 1994. Carnival ships cruise from the west coast of Mexico throughout the Caribbean eastward to the Bahamas. Known as the "Fun Ships," they dazzle passengers with an endless variety of daytime activities and nighttime entertainment.

Carnival Cruise Lines
Carnival Place
3655 NW 87th Avenue
Miami, FL 33178-2428
(800) 327-7373

---

* All destinations are subject to change without notice.

Ship: *Fantasy*
Number of Crew: 920
Number of Passengers: 2,048
Destination: Bahamas

Ship: *Mardi Gras*
Number of Crew: 508
Number of Passengers: 906
Destination: Bahamas

Ship: *Carnivale*
Number of Crew: 550
Number of Passengers: 950
Destination: Bahamas

Ship: *Tropicale*
Number of Crew: 550
Number of Passengers: 1,022
Destination: Caribbean

Ship: *Festivale*
Number of Crew: 612
Number of Passengers: 1,146
Destination: Caribbean

Ship: *Jubilee*
Number of Crew: 670
Number of Passengers: 1,486
Destination: Mexico

Ship: *Celebration*
Number of Crew: 670
Number of Passengers: 1,486
Destination: Caribbean

Ship: *Holiday*
Number of Crew: 660
Number of Passengers: 1,452
Destination: Caribbean

Who's Hiring?—Where to Apply

Ship: *Ecstasy*
Number of Crew: 920
Number of Passengers: 2,044
Destination: Caribbean

Chandris Celebrity Cruises
Part of the Chandris cruise companies, this line caters to the premium (upscale) market. The ships, *Meridian*, *Horizon*, and *Zenith*, cruise the eastern and western Caribbean, and during the spring and summer sail to Bermuda.

Chandris Celebrity Cruises
5200 Blue Lagoon Drive
Miami, FL 33136
(305) 262-6677

Ship: *Horizon*
Number of Crew: 642
Number of Passengers: 1,354
Destinations: Caribbean, Bermuda

Ship: *Meridian*
Number of Crew: 580
Number of Passengers: 1,106
Destinations: Caribbean, Bermuda

Ship: *Zenith*
Number of Crew: 657
Number of Passengers: 1,374
Destination: Caribbean

Chandris Fantasy Cruises
Part of the Chandris cruise companies, this line offers smaller ships catering to more value-oriented customers. It also offers more destinations, including cruises to Mexico, Europe, and South America. Cruises vary in length from a few days up.

Chandris Fantasy Cruises
5200 Blue Lagoon Drive
Miami, FL 33136
(305) 262-6677

Ship: *Amerikanis*
Number of Crew: 400
Number of Passengers: 617
Destination: Caribbean

Ship: *The Azur*
Number of Crew: 340
Number of Passengers: 660
Destination: Mediterranean

Ship: *Britanis*
Number of Crew: 532
Number of Passengers: 926
Destination: Bahamas, South America, Caribbean

Ship: *The Victoria*
Number of Crew: 330
Number of Passengers: 548
Destination: Caribbean, Mediterranean, Europe

Club Med
The company that owns the Club Med resorts around the world built its first cruise ship, the *Club Med I*, in 1990. The ship is the largest sailing ship afloat, but it is designed more as a private yacht for the 386 guests aboard. It sails in the Caribbean and the Mediterranean, offering a sports-oriented cruise with a taste of France. The *Club Med 2* is designed exactly like its sister ship; it visits the South Pacific islands of Tahiti and French Polynesia.

Club Med
40 West 5/th Street
New York, NY 10019
(212) 977-2100

Ship: *Club Med 1*
Number of Crew: 190
Number of Passengers: 386
Destinations: Caribbean, Transatlantic, Mediterranean

Ship: *Club Med 2*
Number of Crew: 190
Number of Passengers: 386
Destination: South Pacific

Commodore Cruise Line
The "Happy Ships" offer affordable seven-day cruises to the Caribbean and Mexico. Commodore's ships are mid-size and offer a great value in cruising to tropical adventure-seekers. Commodore is a division of Effjohn International.

Commodore Cruise Line
800 Douglas Road
Coral Gables, FL 33134
(305) 529-3000

Ship: *Enchanted Isle*
Number of Crew: 350
Number of Passengers: 737
Destination: Caribbean

Ship: *Enchanted Seas*
Number of Crew: 350
Number of Passengers: 744
Destination: Caribbean

Ship: *Caribe*
Number of Crew: 350
Number of Passengers: 875
Destination: Caribbean

Costa Cruise Line
Costa operates a fleet of ships around the world but is currently entering the luxury end of the market with its "EuroLuxe Cruises." The *CostaClassica*, *CostaAllegra*, and *CostaRomantica* provide European style and service in exquisite surroundings. The *CostaClassica*, at $325 million, is one of the most expensive cruise ships ever built.

Costa Cruise Line
World Trade Center Building
80 SW 8th Street
Miami, FL 33130-3097
(305) 358-7325

Ship: *CostaClassica*
Number of Crew: 650
Number of Passengers: 1,300
Destination: Caribbean, Transatlantic, Mediterranean

Ship: *CostaAllegra*
Number of Crew: 450
Number of Passengers: 804
Destination: Greece

Ship: *Carla Costa*
Number of Crew: 370
Number of Passengers: 748
Destination: Mediterranean

Ship: *Costa Marina*
Number of Crew: 385
Number of Passengers: 772
Destination: Caribbean, Mediterranean

Ship: *Costa Riviera*
Number of Crew: 500
Number of Passengers: 984
Destination: Caribbean

Ship: *Danae*
Number of Crew: 250
Number of Passengers: 404
Destination: Mediterranean

Ship: *Enrico Costa*
Number of Crew: 300
Number of Passengers: 700
Destination: Greece

Ship: *Eugenio Costa*
Number of Crew: 475
Number of Passengers: 400
Destination: Mediterranean

Crown Cruise Line

Crown offers deluxe and intimate seven-day cruises from Palm Beach to the Caribbean. In the fall months, the *Crown Monarch* and *Crown Jewel* provide the opportunity to witness the changing colors of the leaves on seven-day cruises to New England and Canada. Crown is a division of Effjohn International.

Crown Cruise Line
800 Douglas Road
Coral Gables, FL 33134
(305) 529-3000

Ship: *Crown Monarch*
Number of Crew: 190
Number of Passengers: 530
Destinations: Canada/New England, Bermuda, Caribbean

Ship: *Crown Jewel*
Number of Crew: 300
Number of Passengers: 820
Destinations: Caribbean, Canada, Bermuda

Crystal Cruises

Crystal offers experienced cruisers the opportunity to see the world in an environment found on few other ships. Its new $200 million ship, the *Crystal Harmony*, spoils its passengers with large penthouses (many with verandas), à la carte restaurants, and Las Vegas–style gambling. The ship, rated 5 stars plus, sails to the Caribbean and to ports in Europe, South America, and the South Pacific.

Crystal Cruises
2121 Avenue of the Stars
Los Angeles, CA 90067
(213) 785-9300

Ship: *Crystal Harmony*
Number of Crew: 545
Number of Passengers: 960
Destinations: World

Cunard Line

Cunard is one of the oldest cruise lines, originating in the 1840s. Its flagship, the *Queen Elizabeth 2*, makes regular transatlantic crossings in addition to cruises to the Caribbean, Canada, Bermuda, and Europe. In winter, the *QE2* also sails on a 107-day cruise around the world. The line also owns two classic cruise ships acquired in 1982, *Sagafjord* and *Vistafjord*; two yacht-like ships, *Sea Goddess I* and *Sea Goddess II*, purchased in 1986; and two less-pricey ships, *Countess* and *Princess*.

Cunard Line
555 Fifth Avenue
New York, NY 10017
(212) 880-7500

Ship: *Queen Elizabeth 2*
Number of Crew: 1,025
Number of Passengers: 1,864
Destinations: World

Ship: *Sagafjord*
Number of Crew: 320
Number of Passengers: 618
Destinations: World

Ship: *Vistafjord*
Number of Crew: 390
Number of Passengers: 772
Destinations: World

Ship: *Sea Goddess I*
Number of Crew: 89
Number of Passengers: 118
Destinations: Caribbean, Europe, Mediterranean

Ship: *Sea Goddess II*
Number of Crew: 89
Number of Passengers: 117
Destinations: Far East, Europe, Mediterranean

Ship: *Cunard Princess*
Number of Crew: 350
Number of Passengers: 802
Destination: Mediterranean

STEAMBOATIN' TIMES
Delta Queen and Mississippi Queen

DAILY LOG OF THE LEGENDARY AMERICAN VACATION

Wednesday   On Board The Mississippi Queen   May 29, 1991

CRUISIN' THE MIGHTY MISSISSIPPI
Good Morning! Good Morning!

• • • **MEAL TIMES** • • •

6:45 AM-8:30 AM Open Seating Breakfast
  Dining Saloon, featuring "a la carte" menu orders.
6:45 AM-9:00 AM "Bountiful Breakfast Buffet"
  Grand Saloon
11:30 AM First Seating Lunch - Dining Saloon
11:30 AM-2:00 PM Light Lunch Buffet
  Grand Saloon
1:30 PM Main Seating Lunch - Dining Saloon
5:45 PM Dinner - A Seating
6:15 PM Dinner - B Seating
8:00 PM Dinner - C Seating
8:30 PM Dinner - D Seating

Dinner music provided by Mr. Dan Perman.
11:00 AM-5:00 PM - Hot Dogs and fixin's, Soft
Serve Ice Cream - Calliope Bar

ALL BARS - DRINK OF THE DAY
"Pina Colada" available in Souvenir Glass

• • • **MOVIE TIMES** • • •
(In the Theater - Lower Deck)

10:00 AM "Steamboat Bill, Jr." (69 min.)
12:30 PM P.B.S. The Civil War: "The Cause-1861"
  (99 min.)
2:30 PM "Life On The Mississippi" (115 min.)
9:45 PM "7 Brides for 7 Brothers" (102 min.)

• • • **TODAY'S ACTIVITIES** • • •

8:15 AM "Riverlorian River Chat" If you would like to find out where we are and where we're going, join our Riverlorian, Jill Turner in the Grand Saloon. (The 'Riverlorian River Chat' can also be heard on Channel "B" in your cabin.)
8:45 AM "Bridge Players Wanted" Bridge players and those passengers who have traveled with us previously on either the Mississippi Queen or the Delta Queen please sign up with your Passenger Service Representative at the Passenger Service Representative Desk in the Forward Cabin Lounge.
9:00 AM "Helpful Hints For Shore Stops" Planning to go ashore on tour, for shopping, or for a refreshing walk? Join Tour Manager, Susan Shea, in the Grand Saloon for an informative and entertaining talk covering your tours and exciting activities ashore. We suggest at least one member of each party attend for important information.
9:30 AM "Walk a Mississippi Mile" Ray is waiting for you at the Calliope Bar to sign you up for a morning walk around the Deck. Eight laps equal one mile.
10:15 AM LET'S GET ACQUAINTED! A chance to meet your fellow Steamboaters and the Staff with fun, prizes and surprises. In the Grand Saloon.

Continued on page 8

Welcome Aboard
Champagne Reception

CAPTAIN GARLAND SHEWMAKER
cordially invites his passengers
to this welcome.
In the Grand Saloon.

4:45 PM   6:00 PM
First Seating   Main Seating

From Page 1

11:00 AM If you've ever wanted to tell someone to go fly a kite, now is your chance. Meet Mike at the Calliope Bar to fly your very own kite. Fly the "Highest Kite" and receive an award.
11:30 AM "Victorian Parlor Crafts" Sheri demonstrates how you can indulge in Victorian Parlor Crafts in the Paddlewheel Lounge, for Main Seating passengers.
12:30 PM "MIGHTY MISSISSIPPI QUEEN STEAMBOAT RACES" It's time to place bets on your favorite boat, in the Grand Saloon. With the roll of the dice - THEY'RE OFF down the river to the PAYOFF !! BAR - DRINK SPECIALS: "Bloody Mary and Hurricane"
1:30 PM "Victorian Parlor Crafts" Paddlewheel Lounge, for First Seating passengers.
2:30 PM "Informal Cards Get-Together" In the Paddlewheel Lounge.
2:45 PM "Welcome to the Mighty Mississippi" Our Riverlorian Jill has an interesting slide presentation on 'Ol Man River' in the Grand Saloon. Discover the Mississippi and its role in forming the history, legend, and folklore of the United States of America.
5:00 PM PADDLEWHEEL MUSIC "Music! Music! Music!" It's time for riverboat music in the Paddlewheel Lounge with Molly Kaufmann and Mike Hashem.
5:00 PM-7:00 PM Happy Hour Specials in all cocktail lounges. Join us for an attitude adjustment. Hors D'Oeuvres are served in the Paddlewheel Lounge.
6:45 PM The Library will be closed until 9:45 PM.

7:00 PM   8:30 PM
Main Seating   First Seating

• • • **SHOWTIME** • • •
"SAY IT WITH MUSIC"

A Chance to dance from coast-to-coast without leaving the room!
Come Dance or just Listen.
In the Grand Saloon.

10:15 PM
• • • **THE LATE SHOW** • • •

IN CONCERT
"Pamela Dudley . . . . . Vocalist Supreme"
accompanied by . . Dan Forman
In the Grand Saloon

11:00 PM
• • • **PADDLEWHEEL LOUNGE** • • •
"THE LATE LATE SHOW"
with

Mike Hashem . . . . Banjoist Supreme
Molly Kaufmann . . . Pianist Extra-ordinaire
and special guest.. Sheri Conner

All you "Nite Owl's" join Molly and Mike for their piano and vocals of Molly Kaufmann. This is "The Place" to be for all First Seating passengers.
8:00 PM "Come Dancin'" First class pre-recorded music summons your happy feet to join our Dance Hosts Dick and James on the Grand Saloon dance floor.
7:15 PM PADDLEWHEEL CORDIAL HOUR Enjoy the piano and vocals of Molly Kaufmann. This is "The Place" to be for all First Seating passengers.
12:00 M "Late Night Buffet" Midnight in Mexico - Upper Paddlewheel.

What's to do aboard a Delta Queen steamboat.

Ship: *Cunard Countess*
Number of Crew: 350
Number of Passengers: 796
Destination: Caribbean

Delta Queen Steamboat Company
This company offers a truly different cruising experience. Founded by the Green family in 1890, the cruise line operates two authentic paddlewheelers (one a National Historic Landmark) on three- to twelve-night voyages up the Mississippi and Ohio Rivers, visiting New Orleans, Chattanooga, Nashville, Memphis, Louisville, Pittsburgh, St. Paul, St. Louis, and Cincinnati. The cruises provide a unique look into the Deep South and America's heartland. Passengers enjoy a taste of history Mark Twain–style.

Delta Queen Steamboat Company
30 Robin Street Wharf
New Orleans, LA 70130-1890
(504) 586-0631

Ship: *Mississippi Queen*
Number of Crew: 154
Number of Passengers: 404
Destination: U.S. rivers

Ship: *Delta Queen*
Number of Crew: 74
Number of Passengers: 176
Destination: U.S. rivers

Diamond Cruise
Owned by a company in Finland but managed and marketed by Radisson Hotels in the U.S., the *Radisson Diamond* can be called nothing short of revolutionary. It is a twin-hulled ship, compared to the single hull of all

other ships, and is designed to serve the corporate meeting and incentive markets rather than leisure cruise passengers. Its design provides a much smoother ride than conventional cruise ships; and its state-of-the-art equipment, including telecommunications, video, and sound and satellite systems, further differentiates it from other ships.

Diamond Cruise
2875 NE 191st Street
North Miami Beach, FL 33180
(305) 932-3388

Ship: *Radisson Diamond*
Number of Crew: 180
Number of Passengers: 354
Destinations: Mediterranean, Caribbean

Dolphin Cruise Line
Dolphin includes a fleet of three smaller ships offering diverse itineraries. Because of their size, the ships can offer more personalized service.

Dolphin Cruise Line
901 South America Way
Miami, FL 33132
(305) 358-5122

Ship: *OceanBreeze*
Number of Crew: 400
Number of Passengers: 388
Destinations: Panama Canal, Caribbean, South America

Ship: *SeaBreeze*
Number of Crew: 350
Number of Passengers: 840
Destination: Caribbean

Ship: *Dolphin IV*
Number of Crew: 280
Number of Passengers: 588
Destination: Bahamas

Epirotiki Lines
Epirotiki, almost 150 years old, began as a trading ship company. It pioneered passenger cruising in the Aegean Sea in 1954 and has since grown to become the largest cruise operator in the Mediterranean.

Epirotiki Lines
551 Fifth Avenue
New York, NY 10176
(212) 949-7273

Ship: *World Renaissance*
Number of Crew: 235
Number of Passengers: 450
Destination: Greece

Ship: *Argonaut*
Number of Crew: 90
Number of Passengers: 166
Destination: Greece

Ship: *Pallas Athena*
Number of Crew: 375
Number of Passengers: 746
Destinations: Greece, Mediterranean

Ship: *Neptune*
Number of Crew: 97
Number of Passengers: 190
Destination: Greece

Ship: *Jason*
Number of Crew: 112
Number of Passengers: 268
Destinations: Greece, Mediterranean

Ship: *Odysseus*
Number of Crew: 190
Number of Passengers: 452
Destinations: Greece, Mediterranean

Ship: *Triton*
Number of Crew: 350
Number of Passengers: 670
Destination: Greece

Ship: *Orpheus*
Number of Crew: 110
Number of Passengers: 288
Destinations: Greece, Mediterranean

Holland America Line

Holland America is now a subsidiary of Carnival Cruise Lines, but it caters to an entirely different market. Through its four ships, staffed by Dutch and Indonesian crews, it serves the luxury market throughout the world. In Alaska and the Pacific Northwest a subsidiary, Westours, is the largest and most experienced tour company. It owns a fleet of deluxe motorcoaches, excursion boats, luxury rail cars, hotels, and inns.

Holland America Line
300 Elliott Avenue West
Seattle, WA 98119
(206) 281-3535

Ship: *Rotterdam*
Number of Crew: 603
Number of Passengers: 1,070
Destinations: World

Ship: *Nieuw Amsterdam*
Number of Crew: 542
Number of Passengers: 1,214
Destinations: Alaska, Panama Canal, Caribbean, West Coast of Mexico and United States

Ship: *Noordam*
Number of Crew: 542
Number of Passengers: 1,214
Destinations: Alaska, Panama Canal, Caribbean, West Coast of Mexico and United States

Ship: *Westerdam*
Number of Crew: 615
Number of Passengers: 1,494
Destinations: Alaska, Panama Canal, Caribbean, West Coast of Mexico and United States

Majesty Cruise Line

Majesty is a new cruise line that offers three- and four-day cruises to the Bahamas. Its first ship, the $220 million *Royal Majesty*, offers a large number of smokefree cabins and a smokefree dining room. In addition to the Bahamas, the ship visits a private island, Royal Isle, and Key West, Florida.

Majesty Cruise Line
901 South America Way
Miami, FL 33132
(305) 358-5122

Ship: *Royal Majesty*
Number of Crew: 500
Number of Passengers: 1,056
Destination: Bahamas

Norwegian Cruise Line

From one ship in 1966, NCL has grown to a fleet of eight ships and is now the official cruise line of the NFL Players Association, the National Basketball Association, the Football and Basketball Halls of Fame, and Universal Studios in Florida and Hollywood. Sports- and entertainment-oriented theme cruises are offered on most ships, from the intimate *Starward* to the three-football-fields-long S.S. *Norway*. NCL was a '60s pioneer of the one-class cruising concept.

Norwegian Cruise Line
95 Merrick Way
Coral Gables, FL 33134
(305) 447-9660

Ship: *Dreamward*
Number of Crew: 483
Number of Passengers: 1,246
Destination: Caribbean, Bahamas, Bermuda

Ship: *Windward*
Number of Crew: 483
Number of Passengers: 1,246
Destination: Caribbean

Ship: *Norway*
Number of Crew: 870
Number of Passengers: 2,044
Destinations: Caribbean, Bahamas

Ship: *Southward*
Number of Crew: 320
Number of Passengers: 754
Destinations: West Coast of United States

Ship: *Westward*
Number of Crew: 325
Number of Passengers: 829
Destinations: Mexico, Bermuda, Caribbean

Ship: *Seaward*
Number of Crew: 624
Number of Passengers: 1,534
Destinations: Caribbean, Bahamas

A classic cruise ship, the S.S. Norway *of Norwegian Cruise Lines.*

Ship: *Starward*
Number of Crew: 315
Number of Passengers: 758
Destination: Caribbean

Ship: *Sunward*
Number of Crew: 325
Number of Passengers: 804
Destination: Bahamas

Oceanic Cruises
Oceanic's small ship, the *Oceanic Grace*, gives its passengers a taste of the Orient. Formerly visiting only the coastal cities of Japan, the ship now visits port cities in China, Korea, and eastern Russia. A bilingual staff and technological innovations to insure smooth sailing make cruising on the *Oceanic Grace* a memorable experience.

Oceanic Cruises
5757 West Century Boulevard
Los Angeles, CA 90045
(213) 215-0191

Ship: *Oceanic Grace*
Number of Crew: 70
Number of Passengers: 120
Destination: Far East

Paquet French Cruises
Through its acquisition of Ocean Cruise Lines and Pearl Cruises in 1990, Paquet has grown to a three-ship fleet. Founded in 1860, the line moved gradually into the passenger cruise industry. The *Mermoz* is the only traditional French luxury liner afloat, marked by its yacht-like atmosphere and fine French cuisine. Ocean Cruise Line's *Ocean Princess* sails from the icy waters of Antarctica to the icy waters of Europe, and Pearl's *Ocean Pearl* is a staple of the Far East market.

Paquet Cruises
1510 SE 17th Street
Ft. Lauderdale, FL 33316
(305) 764-3500

Ship: *Mermoz*
Number of Crew: 320
Number of Passengers: 530
Destinations: Caribbean, Scandinavia, Europe, Mediterranean, Greece

Ship: *Ocean Princess*
Number of Crew: 250
Number of Passengers: 460
Destinations: Europe, South America, Transatlantic

Ship: *Ocean Pearl*
Number of Crew: 232
Number of Passengers: 480
Destinations: Far East, South Pacific

Premier Cruise Lines
Premier is the official cruise line of Walt Disney World and the leader in year-round family cruising. Because of its association with Disney, Mickey, Donald, Goofy, and other characters can be found on every ship; and many passengers combine their cruise with a three- to four-day stay in Orlando. Premier's distinctive big red boats sail not only to Nassau in the Bahamas, but also to lesser known out islands in the Abacos such as Green Turtle Cay, Man-o-war Cay, Treasure Cay, and Great Guana Cay.

Premier Cruise Lines
400 Challenger Road
Cape Canaveral, FL 32920
(407) 783-5061

Ship: Star/Ship *Atlantic*
Number of Crew: 535
Number of Passengers: 1,098
Destination: Bahamas

Ship: Star/Ship *Oceanic*
Number of Crew: 565
Number of Passengers: 1,180
Destination: Bahamas

Ship: Star/Ship *Majestic*
Number of Crew: 390
Number of Passengers: 759
Destination: Bahamas

Princess Cruises

Princess may be one of the best-known cruise lines because of its starring role in the television series "The Love Boat." That series introduced cruising to the masses and helped make Princess one of the three largest cruise lines. The line began in 1964 and operated only one ship until it was acquired by the British shipping concern P and O. By 1984 it operated four ships, and it added three more with the purchase of Sitmar Cruises in 1988. Three new ships followed in three years, bringing the fleet to a total of nine ships offering the most international itineraries of any cruise line.

Princess Cruises
10100 Santa Monica Boulevard
Los Angeles, CA 90067
(213) 553-1770

Ship: *Crown Princess*
Number of Crew: 696
Number of Passengers: 1,590
Destinations: Caribbean, Bahamas

Ship: *Dawn Princess*
Number of Crew: 430
Number of Passengers: 890
Destinations: Mexico, Panama Canal, Caribbean, Bahamas, Alaska

Ship: *Fair Princess*
Number of Crew: 500
Number of Passengers: 890
Destinations: Mexico, Alaska

Ship: *Island Princess*
Number of Crew: 350
Number of Passengers: 610
Destinations: Mexico, Hawaii, Caribbean, Far East, Alaska, South Pacific, South America

Who's Hiring?—Where to Apply

Ship: *Star Princess*
Number of Crew: 600
Number of Passengers: 1,470
Destinations: Caribbean, Transatlantic, Mediterranean

Ship: *Pacific Princess*
Number of Crew: 350
Number of Passengers: 610
Destinations: Far East, Alaska, South Pacific, Hawaii, Caribbean, South America, Panama Canal

Ship: *Regal Princess*
Number of Crew: 696
Number of Passengers: 1,590
Destinations: Panama Canal, Caribbean, Mexico, Bahamas, Alaska

Ship: *Royal Princess*
Number of Crew: 500
Number of Passengers: 1,200
Destinations: Panama Canal, Europe, Mediterranean, Caribbean, New England, East Coast of United States

Ship: *Sky Princess*
Number of Crew: 535
Number of Passengers: 1,200
Destinations: Mexico, Caribbean, Panama Canal, Alaska

Regency Cruises

Regency sails to diverse areas despite its status as a smaller cruise line. Its three ships sail everywhere from Alaska to Hawaii, around the tip of South America up to New England and Canada. The crew is predominantly European, featuring French chefs.

Regency Cruises
260 Madison Avenue
New York, NY 10016
(212) 972-4774

Ship: *Regent Star*
Number of Crew: 450
Number of Passengers: 950
Destinations: Caribbean, Panama Canal, Alaska

Ship: *Regent Sun*
Number of Crew: 390
Number of Passengers: 836
Destinations: Caribbean, Canada/New England

Ship: *Regent Sea*
Number of Crew: 365
Number of Passengers: 729
Destinations: Caribbean, Mexico, Alaska, Panama Canal, Hawaii, South America

Renaissance Cruises

Renaissance offers a unique cruising option, featuring eight yacht-sized ships sailing to many ports other cruise ships don't visit. Because the ships were designed with a very shallow draft, they can sail into remote ports. The result is a chance to see some seldom-visited places in an atmosphere of intimate elegance.

Renaissance Cruises
1800 Eller Drive
PO Box 350307
Ft. Lauderdale, FL 33335-0307
(305) 463-0982

Ship: *Renaissance I*
Number of Crew: 67
Number of Passengers: 100
Destination: Caribbean

Ship: *Renaissance II*
Number of Crew: 67
Number of Passengers: 100
Destinations: Mediterranean, Greece, Europe

Ship: *Renaissance III*
Number of Crew: 67
Number of Passengers: 100
Destinations: Caribbean, Mediterranean, Greece

Ship: *Renaissance IV*
Number of Crew: 67
Number of Passengers: 100
Destinations: Mediterranean, Greece

Ship: *Renaissance V*
Number of Crew: 72
Number of Passengers: 100

Ship: *Renaissance VI*
Number of Crew: 72
Number of Passengers: 100
Destinations: Mediterranean, Greece, Europe

Ship: *Renaissance VII*
Number of Crew: 72
Number of Passengers: 100
Destinations: Mediterranean, Greece, Europe, Caribbean

Royal Caribbean Cruise Line

Consistently rated one of the top cruise lines by passengers and the industry, Royal Caribbean cruises to more places than just the Caribbean. It also offers three-, four-, seven-, eight-, ten-, and twelve-night cruises to Alaska, Bermuda, Europe, and Mexico. Founded in 1969, the company has rapidly grown to a fleet of nine award-winning ships, including three megaliners, the *Monarch of the Seas*, the *Majesty of the Seas*, and the *Sovereign of the Seas*.

Royal Caribbean Cruise Line
1050 Caribbean Way
Miami, FL 33132
(305) 539-6000

Ship: *Song of America*
Number of Crew: 525
Number of Passengers: 1,412
Destinations: Caribbean, Panama Canal, Mexico

Ship: *Sovereign of the Seas*
Number of Crew: 825
Number of Passengers: 2,280
Destination: Caribbean

Ship: *Nordic Prince*
Number of Crew: 425
Number of Passengers: 1,012
Destinations: Caribbean, Bermuda

Ship: *Monarch of the Seas*
Number of Crew: 827
Number of Passengers: 2,354
Destination: Caribbean

Ship: *Song of Norway*
Number of Crew: 425
Number of Passengers: 1,022
Destinations: Caribbean, Europe, Mediterranean

Ship: *Majesty of the Seas*
Number of Crew: 827
Number of Passengers: 2,354
Destination: Caribbean

Who's Hiring?—Where to Apply

Ship: *Sun Viking*
Number of Crew: 320
Number of Passengers: 726
Destinations: Caribbean, Mexico, Alaska, Europe, Bermuda

Ship: *Nordic Empress*
Number of Crew: 685
Number of Passengers: 1,610
Destination: Bahamas

Ship: *Viking Serenade*
Number of Crew: 610
Number of Passengers: 1,514
Destination: Mexico

Royal Cruise Line

Formed in 1971, Royal was voted best cruise line in the world in 1991 by readers of *Conde Nast Traveler* magazine, ranking first in service, restaurant facilities, and stateroom accommodations. It is staffed by a predominantly Greek crew and sails to a wide range of destinations.

Royal Cruise Line
One Maritime Plaza
San Francisco, CA 94111
(415) 956-7200

Ship: *Crown Odyssey*
Number of Crew: 470
Number of Passengers: 1,052
Destinations: Mexico, Hawaii, Mediterranean, Panama Canal, South America, Caribbean

Ship: *Golden Odyssey*
Number of Crew: 200
Number of Passengers: 460
Destinations: Panama Canal, Caribbean, Mexico, Europe, Mediterranean

Ship: *Royal Odyssey*
Number of Crew: 410
Number of Passengers: 765
Destinations: Far East, South Pacific, Alaska, Hawaii, Mexico, Panama Canal, Canada

Royal Viking Line

Royal Viking calls at six of the seven continents. Whereas most cruise lines have proceeded with the rapid addition of ships in the past few years, Royal Viking has reduced its fleet to concentrate on offering a more exclusive product. The original fleet, begun in 1970, was transferred in 1991 to NCL, another company owned by Royal Viking's parent, Kloster Cruise Limited. That leaves the *Royal Viking Sun*, introduced in 1988, and the all-suite *Royal Viking Queen*, delivered in 1992. Together they offer upscale cruises from ten to ninety-nine days to ports around the world.

Royal Viking Line
95 Merrick Way
Coral Gables, FL 33134
(800) 422-8000

Ship: *Royal Viking Sun*
Number of Crew: 460
Number of Passengers: 740
Destination: World

Ship: *Royal Viking Queen*
Number of Crew: 142
Number of Passengers: 212
Destinations: Transatlantic, Panama Canal, Mexico, Europe, Scandinavia

Seabourn Cruise Line

Seabourn, founded in 1987, has three unique features: All of its cabins are suites, it has its own self-contained watersports marina, and its crew provides exceptional service but does not accept tips.

> Seabourn Cruise Line
> 55 Francisco Street
> San Francisco, CA 94133
> (415) 391-7444
>
> Ship: *Seabourn Pride*
> Number of Crew: 140
> Number of Passengers: 204
> Destination: World
>
> Ship: *Seabourn Spirit*
> Number of Crew: 140
> Number of Passengers: 204
> Destinations: Mediterranean, South Pacific

Seawind Cruise Line

Seawind is a recent product of the multibillion-dollar Swedish travel conglomerate Nordisk AB. Its one ship, the *Seawind Crown*, serves a market virtually ignored by the other lines: the southern Caribbean. Based in Aruba, it visits Curaçao, Caracas, Grenada, Barbados, and St. Lucia.

> Seawind Cruise Line
> 1750 Coral Way
> Coral Gables, FL 33134
> (305) 854-7800
>
> Ship: *Seawind Crown*
> Number of Crew: 325
> Number of Passengers: 632
> Destination: Caribbean

Seven Seas Cruise Line

Seven Seas offers one ship to a discriminating clientele. The ship prides itself on a high level of personal service with a strict no-tipping policy. It visits Alaska in the summer and the Orient in the winter.

Seven Seas Cruise Line
555 West Hastings Street
Vancouver, B.C. V6B4N5
(604) 682-7270

Ship: *Song of Flower*
Number of Crew: 144
Number of Passengers: 216
Destinations: Alaska, Far East

Sun Line Cruises
Staffed by a Greek crew, Sun Line was one of the first to enter the luxury market in the 1950s. Its three ships offer a large number of outside cabins, spa cuisine, and top-rated entertainment.

Sun Line Cruises
1 Rockefeller Plaza
New York, NY 10020
(212) 397-6400

Ship: *Stella Solaris*
Number of Crew: 310
Number of Passengers: 620
Destinations: Mediterranean, South America, Caribbean

Ship: *Stella Oceanis*
Number of Crew: 140
Number of Pax: 280
Destination: Mediterranean

Ship: *Stella Maris*
Number of Crew: 110
Number of Passengers: 180
Destination: Mediterranean

A Typical Day as an Entertainer

There is no such thing as a "typical" day for an entertainer. Each day brings it own challenges and rewards, because each week you are working with a new set of passengers.

There are two kinds of entertainers on cruise ships, the staff entertainer and the headliner. The staff member performs and does many other duties, whereas the headliner is flown in to perform. Thus, a headliner's day is very relaxed, while a staff entertainer's day can sometimes be a whirlwind of activity.

As a staff entertainer, the busiest days are the days at sea. A day may begin with an 8:30 a.m. exercise class where you are the instructor. Before you can take a shower, you must rush to horse racing at 10:00, a quick rehearsal at 11:00, and lunch at noon.

After lunch you finally have time for that shower before assisting with bingo at 3:00. You may have to change and go to a formal cocktail party before dinner, and then finally, your moment—actually entertaining! But lest you think the workday is over then, on some sea days you may have to perform a midnight special.

Days in port vary. Staff entertainers take turns doing some tours with the passengers, but usually the days are yours.

If you add up all the hours, individually, it would probably equal a regular workweek, but that does not include rehearsal time. Also, working where you live means you are always at work. If you are relaxing and passengers need assistance, their needs come before your own. Also, as an entertainer you are very recognizable, which some-

> times makes the job difficult. It is definitely a job for people who love people. It can be very challenging, but it is very rewarding when people tell you that you have given them the vacation of a lifetime.
> Juliann Pugh

Windstar Cruises

Windstar was the first to give cruises a sailing option. Its ships are powered by four-masted computer-directed sails and take passengers to large and small ports in French Polynesia, the Caribbean, and the Mediterranean. Their small size and unregimented schedule make for a unique cruising experience.

Windstar Cruises
300 Elliott Avenue West
Seattle, WA 98119
(206) 281-3535

Ship: *Wind Song*
Number of Crew: 91
Number of Passengers: 148
Destination: South Pacific

Ship: *Wind Star*
Number of Crew: 91
Number of Passengers: 148
Destinations: Caribbean, Mediterranean

Ship: *Wind Spirit*
Number of Crew: 91
Number of Passengers: 148
Destination: Caribbean

World Explorer

For the passenger seeking education plus exploration, this is the line to take. Its one ship, the *Universe*, cruises the waters of Alaska during the summer months and provides lectures on the local culture, geology, and wildlife. The rest of the year the ship serves as a traveling university as part of the University of Pittsburgh's "Semester at Sea" program.

World Explorer
555 Montgomery Street
San Francisco, CA 94111-2544
(415) 391-9262

Ship: *Universe*
Number of Crew: 220
Number of Passengers: 500
Destination: Alaska

CONCESSION ADDRESSES
Concessions hiring for multiple cruise lines:

Beauty and Massage
Coiffure Trans Ocean
1001 North America Way
Miami, FL 33132
(305) 358-9002

Steiners of London
c/o Clive Warshaw
57 South Broadway
Stanmore, Middlesex HA74DU
England

Casino
Atlantic Associates
990 NW 166th Street
Miami, FL 33169
(305) 625-7113

Gift Shop

Allders International
1510 South 17th Street
Ft. Lauderdale, FL 33316
(305) 763-8551

Greyhound Leisure
8052 NW 14th Street
Miami, FL 33126
(305) 592-6460

Photographers

Trans Ocean Photos
New York Cruise Ship Terminal
West 54th Street and 12th Avenue
New York, NY 10019

Ocean Pictures
26 Orchard Road
Southhampton, England S012LT

Other concessions hiring for one or more cruise lines include:

Apollo, Miami (Food & Beverage)
Caribbean Cruise Management, Miami (Entertainment)
Casino Austria, Miami (Casino)
Casino Entertainment Limited, Miami (Casino)
Clerici Cruise Services, Miami (Gift Shop)
Cruise Ship Picture Company, Miami (Photographers)
Heads or Nails, Merritt Island, FL (Beauty)
Marine and Mercantile, Miami (Food & Beverage)
Miller Reich, Miami (Entertainment)
Neptune Photographic, London (Photographers)
Oceanic Leisure, Miami (Casino)
OM Consultants, Ft. Lauderdale (Casino)

Who's Hiring?—Where to Apply

Seachest Associates, Miami (Food & Beverage)
Stellar, Miami (Food & Beverage)
W.H. Smith Hotel Services, Inc., Atlanta (Gift Shop)
Walport International, England (Gift Shop)
Zerbone Catering, Miami (Food & Beverage)

The best way to get up-to-date information on these companies and what department within a cruise line you should apply to is to call the job hotlines now provided by most lines.

Fun in the Life of a Sports Director
- On one cruise, a man charged up to me demanding to know what I was going to do about the condition of the shuffleboard court. He said he had waited nine months to play shuffleboard, and now it wasn't working. There was nothing visibly wrong with the court, so in an effort to make it "work," I simply poured a bucket of water over it. The disks flew on that wet court, and the man was ecstatic.
- I discovered that the golf putting tournament can be hazardous to your health. Some first-timers didn't know the difference between a putt and a swing; if you were holding the flag at the hole, you frequently were left with multiply bruised shins.
- The children's time on deck was quite an experience. Chaos usually reigned, and each kid seemed to have his own set of rules for each game we played.
- The kids from countries other than the U.S. were amazing. Not only did they have an excellent

> grasp of English and their native language, but they usually spoke one other as well. Compare this to most American students, who make it through college without having studied a single foreign language.
>
> Amy Dorn

7

How to Apply

THE COVER LETTER
Now that you know all about the cruise industry, have a specific job in mind, and know where to pursue it, it's time to take action! Applying for a job on a ship is just like applying for a job ashore: You send a letter and a résumé with the hope of receiving an application and invitation to interview in return. The first three parts of this campaign—cover letter, résumé, and application—are covered in this chapter. Interviews are discussed in Chapter 8.

A cover letter is similar to a personal letter except that it is typed, set in a business format, and you definitely hope to gain something from it. If you've never written a cover letter, it is a good idea to get help. The many books on the subject can provide good models, but the best source of help is someone who is an expert at writing and grammar or who has experience in hiring employees for a business. Once you have written your cover letter, get one or more of these people to critique and proofread it for you.

The first rule for writing an attention-getting cover letter is to make sure it is in an acceptable format. You don't want your letter to look stuffy, but you do want it to show that you have some knowledge of business etiquette. Second, the letter should be brief. You're not trying to sell your "whole" self in the cover letter; that's the aim of your résumé. You want to reveal only enough of yourself to interest the reader in reading the résumé. If the letter is long or looks overwhelming, it probably won't be read. You have less than ten seconds to attract interest, so pay close attention to this detail.

Third, state the most important parts of your experience and why you think you're qualified for the job. You have to convince the reader immediately that you're the perfect person. That's all the cover letter is—highlights of what is in your résumé and how they relate to the job.

Fourth, express yourself in a positive, upbeat way. The person reading your letter will be looking for evidence of an outgoing personality, the essential quality each crew member must have. Demonstrate that quality in your writing. Transfer your enthusiasm and desire to work for the company into enthusiasm and desire on their part to hire you.

Fifth, and finally, make sure your grammar and spelling are impeccable. This is where enlisting the help of someone with strong English skills can be beneficial. Another person should proofread the letter to catch any mistakes you might have overlooked. If you're working on a computer, there are programs that can do much of the proofing for you. A flawless cover letter gives you the best chance possible of having a personnel officer continue from your letter to your résumé.

Basic Tips to Remember
1. Type on good-quality paper. You can make an impression over hundreds of other applicants by using linen-finish paper instead of ordinary typing paper.
2. Address the letter to a specific person or job

HOW TO APPLY

title. The importance of this has already been mentioned, but it is essential if your materials are to have any chance of reaching the decision-maker.
3. The letter should be flawless. Grammatical or spelling errors show that you're either illiterate or don't have enough pride to review your work.
4. Keep the letter to one page or less. An exhaustive cover letter only speeds its trip to the wastebasket. The shorter and more to the point it is, the more likely it will be read.
5. Be positive and enthusiastic. Your personality has to come through in your writing until you have the opportunity to communicate it face to face.
6. Provide a reason to read your résumé. The ten seconds a person in Human Resources will give your letter may be your only chance to prove you're worth moving on to the next stage. Your cover letter should hook the reader and generate curiosity to move on to your résumé.
7. Sign it. You can write the most hard-hitting, compelling letter of all, but if you forget to sign it, you lose all the momentum you built up in the reader. Before you seal the envelope, look back one more time to be sure your signature is there.
8. Don't let it look like a form letter. You may be sending essentially the same letter to each line, but don't tell them so. True, it costs less to send out twenty-five photocopied letters and résumés, but it also nearly guarantees that you'll get nothing—especially a job—in return.
9. Leave plenty of white space. Leave at least a one-inch margin on each side so that the page is easy to read.

Sample Cover Letter

123 Calloway Avenue
Atlanta, GA 30303
June 1, 1993

Mrs. Tina Rigdon
Director—Onboard Employment
Caribbean Cruise Line
123 Biscayne Boulevard
Miami, FL 33132

Dear Mrs. Rigdon:

Are you looking for an outgoing person with entertainment experience and an extensive travel background?

My name is Meghan Lee. I will be graduating from Georgia Southern University this May and am interested in working in a cruise staff position on board one of your ships. My experience in singing with two campus groups and as social director of my sorority has given me confidence in both entertaining and planning fun activities for large groups of people.

In addition, I have traveled abroad several times. These trips include a foreign study program with my French class and living in two foreign countries with my father, who is in the military.

I expect to be in Miami on May 15 and would like to arrange a personal interview with you if possible. If this date would be convenient for you, would you please call me at 404-876-5432 to arrange a time?

Sincerely,

Meghan Lee

THE RÉSUMÉ

The possible variations on structuring a résumé are endless, but the goal is the same. You want to show through a formal display of your academic and vocational experience why you are qualified to work on a ship in the position you've specified. Your résumé is a picture of you, what you have done in the past, and what you are capable of in the future. It not only shows your qualifications but also reveals something about your attitude, ambition, persistence, and stability. It is the only thing that can persuade the cruise line to interview you. Its importance, therefore, cannot be overestimated.

As with your cover letter, it is advisable to get professional help with your résumé. If you know someone who interviews or hires people on a regular basis, ask him or her to help you in preparing your résumé and proofreading the finished product. Ask what they look for when considering résumés out of a pile of unknown applicants.

Whether you structure your résumé in a chronological, job skill, or some other format depends on which one allows you to demonstrate your strengths in the briefest but most convincing way. Below are samples of typical formats.

FUNCTIONAL FORMAT

Nicolas Wayne
123 Wildes Avenue
Atlanta, GA 30106
(404) 765-4321

Work Experience
Photography. Staff photographer for high school and college yearbook. Covered all sporting events as well as formal events such as proms and fraternity and sorority dances. Won local Best Photograph Award in 1991.

Sales. Organized first annual Photofair for amateur photographers at Metter University. Attracted over forty-five participants in first year and raised $13,000.

Management. Second lieutenant in collegiate ROTC program. Supervised fifty other cadets in various military and civic activities.

Employers
1988–90 *Times-Union.* Assistant to photographer.

1991–Present. Photographer for college yearbook.

Education
Senior, photography major, at Metter University.

CHRONOLOGICAL FORMAT

> Laura Elizabeth James
> 197 Pamlee Lane
> Jodysburg, GA 34328
> (912) 876-5432

Experience

1992–Present **Scruples**, Atlanta
Store Manager. Manage upscale clothing boutique. Have increased sales by 6 percent by instituting new mail approval program. Organized first fashion show for patrons of mall food court.

1990–1992 **Limited**, Marietta
Assistant Manager. Worked with buyers in selecting best-selling merchandise for store. Handled all employee interviewing, hiring, and scheduling. Achieved

rank of Regional Top Salesperson after only three weeks.

Life's a Beach, Atlanta
Salesperson. Sold swimwear and accessories in innovative retail store.

Education
1987   Galloway High School

References upon request.

AUTHOR'S RÉSUMÉ

Donald R. Kennedy
P.O. Box 593
Metter, GA 30439
Phone (912) 685-2175

Education
Bachelor of Science in Business Administration, Cum Laude, The Citadel, The Military College of South Carolina, 1988. Broad business curriculum including coursework emphasis in all aspects of marketing, management, and communication. Four years ROTC training. Literate in Spanish. Computer-literate in three word processing programs, Lotus 123, and ITEK typesetting.

Business Grade Point Ratio: 3.8. Class Rank: 21/453.

Scholastic Honors
Graduated with Departmental Honors in Business Administration.

Citadel Academic Scholarship: Three-year recipient

Gold Stars for Academic Excellence: Four-semester recipient

Phi Kappa Phi National Honor Society
Who's Who in American Colleges and Universities
Economic Honor Society
Citadel Yearbook, Business Manager
Citadel Marketing Club, President

Work Experience
Royal Caribbean Cruise Line, Purser. Served in direct passenger contact role at front desk, handling or directing all complaints and requests. Managed embarkation desk for processing of 250–300 non-U.S. citizens per cruise. Designed book of collector's stamps, which increased front-desk revenues by $150 per month. Managed cash float of $12,000. (May, 1988–Present)

Charleston Tourism Promotion and Management, Intern. Made national-level sales calls, assisted convention coordinator in managing group meetings, and learned organizational logistics for special events with the Sheraton Charleston Hotel. Learned day-to-day operations and participated in special-events planning for boat tours and dinner cruises with The Spirit of Charleston/Fort Sumter Tour Company. (Spring, 1988)

Carnival Cruise Lines, Cruise Staff. Assisted Cruise Director with activities for 1,300 passengers per week aboard T.S.S. *Festivale.* Disc-jockeyed for Fanta-Z Disco and for private cocktail parties. Sold lottery tickets for Cruise Director. In first two weeks, sold four times more tickets than had ever been sold by a cruise staff member. Produced and marketed Caribbean music tape, which netted $400 extra income per week. (Summer, 1987)

Sitmar Cruise Line, Cruise Staff. Assisted Cruise Director with activities for 1,100 passengers per cruise aboard T.S.S. *Fairsky*. Greeted passengers at "Welcome Aboard" and "Farewell" cocktail parties. Disc-jockeyed for three discos and all cocktail parties. (Summer, 1986)

Norwegian Cruise Line, Cruise Staff. Assisted Cruise Director with deck activities for 800 passengers per week aboard M/S *Starward*. Supervised all teen activities. Disc-jockeyed for two discos and all cocktail parties. (Summer, 1985)

FORMAL APPLICATIONS

When you apply for a job on a cruise line, you have no choice but to wait and hope for an application to be sent to you. If you receive one, you've made it across the first hurdle. It may even be cause for celebration, because it means that the line is at least mildly interested in you.

A cruise line's "official" application is much like any standard employment application. It has fill-in-the-blanks spaces for your name, address, social security number, etc. There are spaces to list your education and your past jobs. It may ask questions about your health and why you want to work on a cruise ship. Fill it out neatly (preferably typed), and return it as quickly as possible.

Reference Sheets and Photos

Two other items that will professionalize your application materials and make it easier to hire you are a list of personal and work references and a photo or two of yourself. References can help a personnel agent do a quick check to verify your résumé.

The photo is actually not an option; it's a must. You should send one with your first application. The lines are very particular about the image their people project, and sending a photo in the first volley cuts out a few weeks' response and request time and makes you immediately available for hire. The photo should be a full body shot, in a natural pose, with you as the sole subject.

These five parts—cover letter, résumé, application, photo, and reference sheet—make up the first two stages of your job-hunting effort. Once you have received and returned an application and are waiting for an interview, you are in the most frustrating part of the job search—the follow-up stage. This, more than anything, can determine whether you or one of the hundreds of other applicants gets the job.

8

How to Follow Up

What can you expect from a cruise line in response to your application materials? Maybe—nothing. People tell me, "I sent letters and résumés to a lot of cruise lines, but I didn't hear anything." After that, they simply gave up and returned to the "9-to-5 grind" they were trying to get away from. They didn't get a job on a cruise ship because they were not committed to getting a job on a cruise ship. They wanted it only if it was easy.

Nobody said it was going to be easy. You can't just get together a list of addresses, type up a résumé, send it off, and expect a job offer a couple of weeks later—even with years of cruise experience. If you really want a job on a cruise ship, you must follow up with determined persistence, constantly keeping your name in front of the appropriate cruise line personnel so that when a job does become available, you are the first person they think of.

Knowing what to expect will keep you from giving up for the wrong reason when you receive little or no response. You will understand that the initial lack of interest is only part of the process and you will be prepared to take the next step. What should you expect? Within two to six weeks after you've done your mass mailing, one of four things will happen.

1. Nothing. When I first applied in the summer after my freshman year of college, I got no response from my first mailing. Most people would have given up at that point. Not to get even a rejection can be discouraging. I just accepted it as best I could and resolved to be even more determined when I applied in the spring. And, of course, when I applied in the spring I did get a different response.
2. You'll get standard rejection letters. Receiving these letters was not much better than the previous zero response, but at least they acknowledged receipt of my materials. They all said basically the same thing, "Thank you for your application, but we regret that we have no positions available at this time." I did write again to say that should the situation change, I would be very interested. But it was not until the second mail campaign in the spring that number three happened.
3. You'll get an application. These are the forms discussed in Chapter 7. As has been said before, just being offered the chance to fill out and return an application is a major milestone; it means that your cover letter and résumé were read and that the person who did so thought you had enough potential to warrant further consideration.
4. You'll get a job offer. This is very unlikely with your first set of applications. It is more likely to come after you've received a few rejection letters. Whatever the case, when you do get an offer, consider yourself fortunate, as there were probably several hundred other people trying for that same position.

Of course, if you receive a job offer, you need only accept it, and your dream is realized. But this chapter is based on the unfortunate probability that that won't happen after your first mailings. That is why you must learn and practice skillful follow-up. It can determine whether you ultimately get a job offer.

Effective Follow-Up

Your follow-up consists of two parts: correspondence and telephone calls. A well-planned campaign utilizing both will significantly improve your chances of getting a job. The question is what should you do and when should you do it? Your first contact, of course, is your cover letter and résumé. If you hear nothing from that in three to four weeks, try calling to say that you had sent a letter and would like to confirm that it was received. This may not be easy, as many cruise lines don't accept phone calls from applicants. But if you do get through and they say they have received it, you're fine. If they don't know who you are or can't find anything from you, offer to send another cover letter and résumé addressed to the person with whom you are speaking. If you get an okay, you've increased your odds.

Three weeks to a month after you've sent in your second letter or they've said they're reviewing your first, it's time to make another contact. Send a short letter stating that you had sent in a résumé a few weeks earlier and just wanted to reaffirm your desire to work for the line should a position become available. This puts your name in front of the personnel department's eyes once more, and it may cause them to pull your résumé out for a second look.

After this second contact, you should do one of two things. If you have accomplished something related to work, such as graduating or getting a promotion, write the cruise line another letter telling them about it. This makes you "even more qualified," and once again they see and read your name. If you've been dealing with a specific person instead of a department, he or she should be getting to know you by now.

If you still haven't heard anything from the line, and it has been over four months, it may now be appropriate to make another phone call asking at what point they clean out their files and whether it would be wise for you to send another résumé. If it has been six months, you should definitely get ready for another mass mailing.

This one will be much like your first one. Again blanket all the lines and companies that hire for your position. Your cover letter and résumé should follow the same format, except that you might mention having applied before and add that you are still very interested in the position.

Once again you go through the same follow-up steps: phone call to make sure the materials were received, another copy if not, a separate letter reaffirming your desire, etc. You continue this cycle until you either get an offer or decide that you would rather do something else. I had gone through the complete cycle twice before giving up and deciding to do something else for my summer job. One week into it, however, I received my first offer—at age eighteen—to work on a ship in the Caribbean.

You might think that the next three years were easier for me, but they weren't. Each time I had to go through at least two cycles of application and rejection before I got hired. So if you're applying for the first time, don't skip the next paragraph.

How to Follow Up

Hanging In There
There's no way to predict whether it will take you one cycle or four before you get a break. What it takes, if you think you are really qualified for a position and could make a valuable contribution, is the persistence to keep on applying and making contact through the steady barrage of negatives you will surely receive. The only time you definitely have no chance of getting a job is when you admit defeat and quit. The longer you try to become known as a persistent, but not pestering, applicant, the more likely it is—solely because of your follow-up—that you will be hired.

A Typical Day as a Teen Counselor
A usual day at sea started around 9 a.m. The teens and I would meet for breakfast at the Veranda Café. Promptly at 9:30, the walk-a-thon would begin. This is part of Royal Caribbean's Ship-Shape fitness program. Each time passengers completed five laps around the ship, they received one Ship-Shape dollar. When they reached five dollars, they could cash them in for a Ship-Shape T-shirt and visor.

Throughout the morning, we would have tournaments: Ping Pong, golf putting, basketball throwing, shuffleboard, and ring tossing. Around noon, we would break for lunch, usually hamburgers and hotdogs at the Veranda Café.

At two o'clock we would continue the tournaments or perhaps have a scavenger hunt. At four o'clock we would lie out on the sun deck for about thirty minutes. That would end the afternoon. We would meet again at 8 p.m. to play games such as Scrabble, cards, bingo, or everyone's favorite—

Win, Cruise, or Draw. Sometimes we would spend a while at the disco. An evening with the teens would end around 10 p.m.

As a teen counselor, it was also my responsibility to walk around deck at night to make sure none of my teens were involved in mischief. Once we discovered a group jumping off the upper deck into the pool on the deck below. After that incident, the pool became our first stop on the nightly rounds.

Days in port were not as busy as those at sea. At certain ports we had organized morning shore excursions for the teens. In St. Thomas, for example, we took them to Coral World, and in Barbados, to the Harrison Caves.

Suzanne Kelley

9

Interviewing for the Job

You may be wondering whether we didn't leave out a step. What about an interview? The good news—if you're one of those people who dread the thought of a high-pressure job interview—is that you may not have to have a personal interview to be hired on a cruise ship.

This is the area where the hiring process differs most from that ashore. If you were applying for a position at a company near where you live, you'd be bound to have at least one personal interview before being hired. Most employers want to judge your appearance and ability to communicate before hiring you.

Cruise lines, however, usually have to skip that convenience. Unless you already live in Miami, New York, or Los Angeles, it's likely that you are several hundred miles away from the cruise line's home offices. The lines hire hundreds of people each year, very few of whom live in those cities, and the cost of flying them in for interviews would be astronomical. Therefore, interviews have to be done in a more economical fashion.

THE TELEPHONE INTERVIEW
The more economical fashion, obviously, is by telephone. That may seem odd, but it is really the only feasible way. It stands to reason, then, that if interviews

are what get people hired, and yours will be on the phone, that one phone call is all-important. The person calling you from the cruise line will already have seen the picture you sent in with your application. Your job now is to convince him or her that you are a great communicator, have an outgoing personality, would treat the passengers like royalty, and are the perfect person for the job.

That is no small order when you have ten minutes or less to present your case. The person calling will probably ask a few routine questions, then give you a chance to ask questions or talk about yourself and your interests. This is not the time to attack with, "How much do you pay?" You don't have an offer yet, so that question is moot.

The problem with the phone interview is that you have no idea when this do-or-die call will come. It might be in the morning before you're up, or in the middle of lunch. You'll pick up the phone, the person on the other end will identify himself as being from so-and-so cruise line, and the rest of the conversation will serve as your interview. Such spontaneity will require fast thinking on your part. You'll have to gather and organize your thoughts quickly, and it is to be hoped that you will have given some thought to what you want to say.

This could be your make-or-break chance. If you receive a phone call, you're already way up on the list of hiring possibilities. Your communication skills and interaction on the phone may be all it takes to bring an offer. The first phone call might just be introductory—but it also could be *the one*. I was hired for my first job one day when I came in from work for lunch. We talked about five minutes; he asked if I could be there in a week, I said yes, and he said you're hired! For my third job, the phone call took a little longer—forty-five minutes—but it too ended with a job offer.

Interviewing for the Job

If you don't get a job offer from this first phone call, don't be discouraged. The cruise line may just be trying to winnow their stack of promising résumés. Handle the phone call without being overanxious. Don't assume you're going to be offered a job and come across as arrogant. Use your best judgment based on the caller's tone, comments, and questions. If you think the conversation is about to end with just "thanks for your time," you might become a little more assertive. Restate your interest in working for the line, reaffirm why you would make a good hire for the job, and ask what the next step is. Thank the person sincerely for calling, and then *write* a personal thank you, showing your appreciation for the call.

Personal Interviews

It is almost certain that you will have one or more phone conversations with Human Resources personnel if they are considering hiring you. Whether or not you have the opportunity to meet with them in person will depend on one of two things:

1. If you are within driving distance of a city where the cruise line has offices, don't pass up the chance to go and talk with someone personally. Nothing can substitute for a face-to-face meeting. How far it is reasonable to drive will be up to you. But the cost of gas should be weighed carefully against the potential advantage gained by a personal interview.
2. If you don't live within driving distance but are willing to fly to an interview, you can probably arrange a meeting. A flight can be expensive, but absorbing the cost yourself will impress the interviewer and possibly give you an edge. You

will also derive the benefits described in the next paragraph.

If you do have a chance to schedule a personal interview, be sure do so. Just having someone see you, talk with you, and know that you have no "weaknesses" that you "forgot" to mention on your application will establish a confidence level. They now know exactly what they're getting.

Your interview will be pretty much what you would expect in an interview ashore. The interviewer will try to put you at ease, then ask a few specific questions. Answer these as succinctly and enthusiastically as possible.

The one question that is sure to come up will be about your availability. As has been mentioned, cruise ships frequently get short notice when a person is leaving a ship, so the position must be filled on equally short notice. If you are free to pick up and go when needed, you have a much better chance of being hired.

When the interviewer has covered all the questions, you'll probably have a chance to ask some of your own. Don't make salary the first one. Although it is a prime concern for anyone, it can wait until you've been offered a job. Do ask any questions that may have come to you during the interview or that you were already prepared to ask.

At the end of the interview, thank the person for his or her time, reassert your desire to work for the line, and ask what will be the next step. Smile and say thank you once again as you leave. Immediately after getting home or to your hotel room, write a thank-you note. If you don't hear anything for a few weeks after your interview, utilize some of the "keep your name in front of them" techniques discussed in the last chapter.

> Cruise Staff Rituals
>
> As a crew member, I enjoyed port days the most. My favorite thing to do was in Barbados. A few of us would go to Shakey's pizza for dinner. Shakey's wasn't the typical brick-and-window building. It was all open air, with wooden decks and shutters and calypso music playing—very Caribbean! We would always order pineapple and Canadian bacon pizza and share a pitcher of Coke or beer.
>
> I loved going to all the islands, having lunch there, and then heading to one of the many gorgeous beaches. The entire Caribbean is so beautiful. My favorite island was Labadee, Royal Caribbean's private island in Haiti. The cruise staff members would try to find a part of the island without passengers and go relax. Hammocks were all over the island, so we would just lounge, sip piña coladas, and take in the beautiful scenery—paradise!
>
> Suzanne Kelley

The following tips may help you in preparing for—and succeeding in—a personal interview.

1. **Know something about the company.** It would be really embarrassing if you were asked where you would most like to work and you named an area where the cruise line doesn't even sail. Study travel agents' brochures, one of the many books on cruise travel, or Chapter 6 of this book, so that you at least know the basic facts about the cruise line with which you're interviewing.
2. **Show a positive attitude.** Say something bad about your past employer or talk about what

you hate most in the world, and you'll kill any chance of being hired. The cruise lines are looking for positive, upbeat people, not sourpusses, even if the latter have a better education or more experience.

3. **Smile**. A bright smile is one way to show your positive attitude. A smile radiates enthusiasm. It can convey the sense of personality and congeniality that the cruise lines seek.
4. **Shake hands firmly**. A weak handshake communicates weakness. It demonstrates shyness and an inability to socialize with strangers. Shake hands firmly with your interviewer and communicate unswerving self-confidence.
5. **Look the person in the eye**. Constantly looking away or down during a conversation is a common signal of shyness or dishonesty. Don't stare, of course. Just make consistent eye contact while listening and speaking to the other person.
6. **Be aware of body language**. Are you slouching? Do you fidget when asked point-blank questions? Your impression on the interviewer could be more important than what you say.
7. **Make your appearance impeccable**. A recent haircut, pressed clothes, and shined shoes are essential to your success in interviews. Failure to display pride in your own appearance means you probably won't display pride in your job once on the ship.
8. **Show your outgoing personality**. Throughout this book we have stressed that the single most important quality you can have or show is an outgoing personality. It is crucial that in every contact with the line, but particularly in an interview, you turn your personality on.

9. **Don't talk too much—or too little**. Talking too little will leave the interviewer knowing no more about you after the interview than before, but talking too much will make you sound arrogant. Walk a fine line between answering questions and telling your whole life story.
10. **Be on time**. Showing up late for a job interview will leave you little or no chance to regain your credibility. Punctuality is important on a cruise ship. If you miss the ship in any port, you risk being left behind—and fired!
11. **Be honest**. If you feel any temptation to "enhance" your experience and qualifications on your résumé, lose it. Lying about your history may help you get hired; but if the truth later comes out or if you are unable to do something you said you could do, you'll end up losing your job and probably any chance of being hired by another line.
12. **Be prepared**. Know what you want to learn from the interview. You are expected to have questions of your own. Asking well-thought-out questions can help your cause. Carrying a notebook is one way to keep organized and also to record key points that come up during the interview.
13. **Be relaxed**. You're in a one-on-one situation with someone who has the power to determine whether or not you get a job, but you don't have to treat it that way. Be relaxed and talk as if you were talking to a friend about an exciting job. An interviewer will try to put you at ease in the first few minutes, but that won't be necessary if you are already calm and self-assured.

EXPLORING CAREERS ON CRUISE SHIPS

The Crystal Court, main entrance of the Seaward. *Beautifully decorated multideck entrances are becoming a standard feature of the new larger cruise ships.*

10

Preparing to Go

ACCEPTING THE JOB

How you might receive a job offer has been discussed in detail. It could come with your first phone call and you're needed in a week, or you might have a personal interview and get several weeks' notice before you start. But it is essential to be prepared when it does come.

Ask any questions that might have an impact on your answer, and then give one. If the offer comes on a first contact with a line or only a week or so before you're needed, your answer may be needed right away. Not being able to give it during the call or at least by the next day could cost you the offer. If you've been thinking positive, you should be prepared for an offer. The only variable other than pay, if you haven't already discussed that, is how long before you have to leave.

If there is plenty of time before you're needed, you might be able to take longer with your decision, and you'll have more time to prepare if you do accept the offer. On two occasions, I was offered a position about three months before it was to be open. I accepted on the phone when the offer was made. But having advance knowledge gave me time to prepare for the months away from home.

WHAT TO PACK

I'm not sure how I knew what to take on board that first job. It may be that since I was attending a military school, I didn't have a lot of the things a college freshmen would have. Or maybe it was because I was a DJ and had so many boxes of records and tapes that I couldn't afford to take much else with me. Whatever the reason, it was a good thing I didn't.

I've mentioned how small the cabins typically are on a cruise ship. Well, the crew cabins can be even smaller. Even though the ship is your new home, it's nothing like moving into an apartment. Your cabin will already be "furnished," so you don't need any decorative accessories. You will be eating in a crew dining room, so there's no need for kitchen equipment.

What you do need is pretty much what you would take if you were a passenger. If you've ever packed for a long vacation with your family, you'll have a good idea of what are the "necessities."

Clothes

Whether you'll need summer clothes or winter clothes depends on the itinerary of your ship. If you are just doing short cruises in the Caribbean, all you'll need for casual wear is beach clothes plus an outfit or two in case you have dinner in port. If your ship sails to Alaska or Scandinavia, you'll need jeans and jackets instead. It is a good idea to discuss this with the person who hires you.

What formal wear you'll need depends on your job. If you are a member of the cruise staff you will almost certainly need a tuxedo or formal evening dress. This is one expense you will incur up front. In addition to formal nights, many lines also have theme and costume nights. You should find out about such special nights and what clothes you'll need.

Most jobs aboard require some type of uniform. This ranges from a Navy-like uniform for officers to blue shirts and white shorts for cruise staff members. The cruise line may provide your uniform, or you may be responsible for part of it.

In deciding what to take, make it only your favorites. You won't find walk-in closets in your cabin, nor two or three chests of drawers. You may have two or three feet of hanging space and two or three drawers. That's it! So plan accordingly. Keep in mind that you'll want to shop in the ports you visit anyway.

Photographic and Entertainment Equipment

If you have a camera, you will definitely want to take it with you. Every place you visit will offer wonderful pictures, and the greatest pleasure comes from being able to write captions and send them home to family and friends. If you are to be sailing in the Caribbean or other warm-water ports, do your best to get an underwater camera to use while scuba diving or snorkeling. If you don't have one, look for one in a duty-free shop on board or in port.

The next category is TVs, VCRs, and stereos. Few people lug a lot of electrical equipment on board when they first go to work on a ship. You shouldn't, either. You don't know if you'll have room in the cabin, or your roommate may already have some. And most important, if you're visiting a port such as St. Maarten, which specializes in entertainment equipment, you can

Norwegian Cruise Lines' "Pleasure Island" in the Bahamas. If you'll be working in the Caribbean, be sure to take plenty of beach and watersports gear with you.

pick up what you want for less than it would cost in the U.S. The downside is that when it's time to leave the ship, you have to figure out how to get your acquisitions home. Some crew members just sell their major appliances to other crew members.

If you have a smaller device such as a Walkman, do take that. It's great for walking on the beach or lying out on deck. A good rule of thumb is that if something won't fit neatly in a suitcase, don't take it.

Books, Pictures, and Personal Items

Since you are making a new home, you need things to keep you busy when you're off and to make your cabin

Preparing to Go

more "homey." Little things like books and pictures of your family and friends can help reduce that, "I'm so far from home" feeling. You may be thinking, "I won't be in the cabin. I'll be out partying anyway." That may be true initially. But once you've seen all the shows and visited all the ports, you'll enjoy just sitting around your cabin and relaxing.

Don't worry about personal items. Almost all ships have a crew store where you can buy basics like razorblades plus things like candy, alcohol, and cigarettes.

Beach and Watersports Gear

If you know that you're sailing to Alaska or northern Europe, you won't need beach accessories. If you're on a ship that has an indoor pool or a heated spa (and your position allows), you may be able to use a swimsuit.

Let's assume, however, that you're on one of the ships sailing to warm-weather ports. You'll surely want to go to the beach, and when you do, there'll be goodies you'll want to take with you. First, of course, is sunscreen, tanning oil, or other protection from the sun. In the Caribbean, South America, Pacific, or Mediterranean, you're closer to the equator, and the sun's rays are much more direct. You can get sunburned in no time. Even if you tan easily, you might want to take extra protection for the open seas.

With all this direct sunshine, you will probably want some good sunglasses. Specially treated lenses are available that provide such good protection that you can look right at the reflected light off the ocean. A pair of these can be handy, especially in such places as Grand Cayman, where the glare off the clear seas can be blinding.

Another accessory that might help you withstand the heat is a minicooler or sports bottle. Whether you pack ice and drinks in the cooler or just fill a squeeze bottle with your favorite drink, you'll enjoy having it on the beach. Of course, if you're sunbathing in front of many Caribbean hotels, there'll be a waiter or waitress to bring you drinks.

The last thing to remember is to have your own towel. This may not be necessary if you're visiting a hotel, but if you're seeking a secluded spot on the beach, the sand is likely to be hot, and you will need something to lie on.

The main watersports gear you might take are a snorkel, a mask, and fins. Snorkeling in the beautiful waters of the Caribbean is an incredible experience, and if you can do it without having to rent equipment, it is an inexpensive but fun thing to do in port. If your ship offers a scuba program, of course, you may get to do much more than snorkel.

Outdoor and Athletic Equipment

Whether you're sailing in cool or warm climates, you'll have a chance to enjoy the ports you visit and participate in activities there. In mountainous regions, you can go hiking, river rafting, or skiing. In warmer regions, you can also go hiking or riding or play golf, tennis, or other sports. To be able to enjoy these sports, you need to take related equipment with you.

For hiking, plan on packing boots, backpack, compass, canteen, binoculars, and so on. Of course, most of the ports you visit will be well populated, so the chance of getting lost or stranded is remote. The limited storage space in your cabin is also a factor to consider when deciding whether to outfit yourself for two-hour walks or week-long wilderness treks.

The golf and tennis opportunities are limitless. Because cruise ships visit popular tourist destinations, it isn't uncommon to find scores of hotels and resorts with golf and tennis courses. If you are an avid player, you will probably want to take your clubs or rackets and keep them in a corner of your cabin.

How I Got My Job as an Entertainer

Getting hired on a cruise ship is different for each person and each position. My first experience was when I had just graduated from college with a degree in fine arts. I wasn't at all sure where I was going or what I was going to do, but I knew I wanted to sing.

On the job notice board in the drama department, I came across a notice for auditions for a revue show for Carnival Cruise Lines.

I called right away and set up an audition time. Armed with a photograph, résumé, and the necessary sheet music, I headed to the audition. The producer was very nice and explained what he was looking for. It was a four-person revue (four-part harmony), and he needed a female with an alto range. I was perfect (I felt)! I sang my heart out and gave it all I had. The song was a comedic number, and he laughed at all the right places. I just knew I had bagged the part! He thanked me repeatedly and said he would call.

Well, he did call—to tell me he had hired another girl. My heart collapsed with disappointment. He told me that shipboard life was very difficult and the quarters were very small and confining. He had chosen someone else, he said, not because she was better, but because she had previously worked with the soprano he had already hired. Because they would have to be roommates on the ship, it seemed best to go with people who already knew each other.

He promised to call me as soon as he had a spot in his next revue. I thought he was just easing me down, but less than three weeks later he did call: The alto he had hired wasn't working out, and could I be ready to sail in two weeks?

The ship hiring process is like that, I have since learned. They may continually tell you no, but one day you will get a call out of the blue saying that you are leaving that weekend. You must be flexible and ready to sail at the drop of a hat. If that isn't your style, shipboard life is not for you.

Juliann Pugh

GETTING TO THE SHIP

At some point during your conversations with cruise line personnel, the issue of how you'll get to the ship should come up. The cruise line may cover this trip for you, or you may be responsible for paying for it. Which is the case will depend on the position you've been hired for and the cruise line's policy. If the subject does not come up well before your departure date, it's okay to bring it up. If you are responsible for your transportation, you want at least to have a chance to buy tickets with an advance discount.

You probably will need to arrive in the departure city at least one day before boarding the ship. You'll need time for the mandatory physical exam and to be fitted for any necessary uniforms. The cruise line will make those arrangements for you. Your excitement that night, knowing what you'll be starting the next day, will make it hard for you to go to sleep!

11

Life on Board

You made it! All the effort, all the persistence paid off. You reached your goal and are on board. Or maybe you haven't started applying yet but want to see what you're working toward? That's great, because having a realistic picture of life as a crew member will help you decide if you really want a job, and also help you adjust to your surroundings once you're on board.

MAKING NEW FRIENDS

The first thing you'll notice is how fast you make friends. There is a strong sense of family among a cruise ship's crew. Because you are a long way from home, the other crew members are the people you see and associate with daily. You will make friends with them rather quickly, living only a few doors apart and being around them all day every day. The fact that the crew includes people from all over the world with their own languages and customs makes the friendships even more fun and interesting.

WHERE YOU LIVE

Your "home" is a cabin, varying in size according to your ship's size and age. Like a mini dorm room, a cabin usually has bunk beds, closet space, a desk, and maybe a few other fixtures. There won't be room for all

LIFE ON BOARD

the possessions you're used to at home. You will have space only for your clothes, toiletries, a radio or small TV, and possibly a few other small items. Your cabin may feel a little cramped at times, but considering that you're paying no rent for it, the small size is not such an inconvenience.

What You Eat

Most ships have separate dining rooms for the groups of crew members. Officers eat in one dining room, cruise staff members in another, and hotel/dining room staff in yet another. The menu varies, depending on the nationalities of the crew members in each dining room. But the higher your rank, the more likely you'll be eating the same cuisine as the passengers. In fact, many officers and cruise staff members eat in the passenger dining room.

The food is excellent; but like anything else, the more you have, the sooner you tire of it. Many crew members, having dined on steak, shrimp, and other fancy foods at sea, can hardly wait to get to port for a hamburger or pizza. Whether or not you can keep snacks in your cabin depends upon the rules of the ship, but most crew members do manage to keep a stash of cookies or other sweets. If your ship has a crew pantry, you may be able to keep food there and also cook when and what you like.

GETTING PAID

There is no set method for this. You may be paid weekly, biweekly, or monthly. You may be paid on the ship or have to wait until you get to port. Most crew members earn a salary, but some, such as the room stewards and waiters, make almost all of their pay from tips given to them by passengers at the end of the cruise.

The S.S. Norway's Roman Spa. Depending on your job, on your day off you may be able to use the ship's elegant facilities.

WORK AND PLAY

Your free time is determined by your job. It you're a cruise staff member, you might work six to eight hours. If you're a waiter or room steward, it may be up to fifteen hours. In either case, however, you have your days off to enjoy the ship and the ports you visit. If you're not working on a day in port, you are free to tour and sightsee. If the ship repeats the same itinerary each cruise, eventually you will get to see all the places the ship visits. Essentially, you are getting paid to see the world.

ON BOARD PRIVILEGES

How and where you spend your time aboard depends on your rank. Officers and many cruise staff members have access to all public areas: the lounges, the shows, the recreation rooms. Members of the hotel and food and beverage staffs usually do not have that access. They are restricted to crew areas except when doing a function for their jobs. Only officers, because of their rank, and cruise staff members, because part of their job is entertaining passengers, are allowed to mingle freely anywhere on the ship.

Basic Necessities
Toiletries and other everyday items can be obtained in one of three ways: You can have them sent from home, you can buy them in ports the ship visits, or you can buy them in the crew store.

Laundry can be done self-service or full service. Almost all ships have laundry facilities that handle the ship's linens. These facilities usually will launder the crew's uniforms and personal garments for a reasonable price. Some newer ships also offer self-service laundry rooms where passengers and crew can wash clothes.

Sending and receiving mail is one of the highlights of life on board. Mail usually comes to the ship in the home port from which it operates. Sending mail is also fun, especially from foreign ports. You can send postcards of the beautiful places you're visiting, using exotic stamps bought from the post offices there.

Alcohol and Drugs
Almost all cruise ships, whether sailing to U.S. or foreign ports, now enforce either an eighteen- or twenty-one-year-old drinking requirement. As a crew member, if you are under the required age, you will find it difficult to obtain alcohol. But that can be advantageous, as it prevents you from spending all you make on drinks.

You may find illegal drugs available among the crew or in the ports you visit. The reasons for avoiding them are serious: Most lines have a strict policy that if you are

Exploring Careers on Cruise Ships

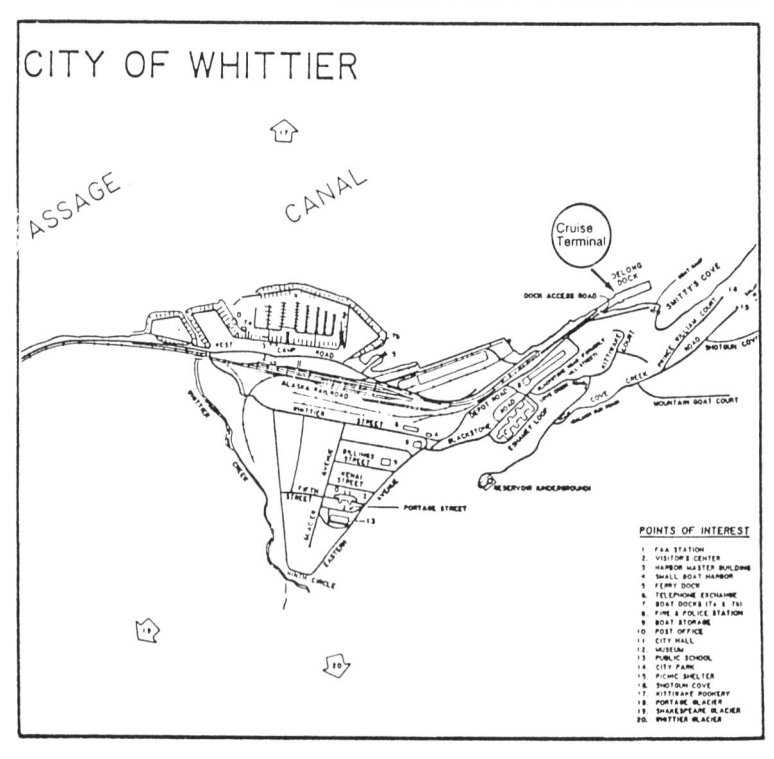

The city of Whittier, Alaska, one of the many ports you may visit on cruises to the Pacific Northwest.

caught with drugs on the ship, you will be terminated immediately and put off in the next port. If you are caught with drugs in a port that your cruise ship visits, your punishment could be worse.

In some countries, dealers sell a person drugs, then collect a reward from the police for turning that person in. And the jails in those countries do not offer the amenities of North American jails, nor are the justice systems as democratically based. Get caught in the wrong country, and you'll be spending more time in paradise than you ever imagined.

HEALTH CARE

Every ship has medical facilities, usually staffed by a doctor and two nurses, but these are not comprehensive medical centers. They have only emergency equipment and first-aid materials. Serious cases are evacuated from the ship. Sophisticated medical care may not be available in the ports you visit either. Dental care is also unavailable on the ship and in some ports, so have any needed work done before you join the ship.

RELIGIOUS SERVICES

Some larger ships employ full-time clergymen to provide religious services for passengers and crew. Others ask passengers who are members of the clergy to lead interdenominational services. If neither is provided on your ship or if you wish to attend a more formal service, you may attend places of worship in the ports you visit.

12

Is It the Right Job for You?

You should have concluded by now that working on a cruise ship is not for everyone. Getting on board and doing well in a job is not as easy as stopping in a retail store at the mall and filling out an application for employment. You have to decide if it's the job for you and if you are the right person for the job. To help you in making this evaluation, here are the four most important questions to consider.

How much do I enjoy working with people? Are you an introvert who prefers working alone, or an extrovert who thrives on contact with other people? If you can't deal with a constant environment of complaints, requests, and questions, you'll hate working on a ship. Passengers expect you to cater to their every whim, and the cruise line expects you to fulfill those expectations. If you enjoy meeting people of different backgrounds, you'll love the ships. You'll learn a valuable skill—the ability to get along with all types of people—that will serve you well in anything you eventually decide to do on land. And you'll be proud when you start getting compliments on passenger cards, "Don, the purser, was so nice and helpful. We had a wonderful time."

Can I stand seasickness and homesickness? There is a quick cure for one, but the other takes months. Most

Trolland, the children's playroom aboard the S.S. Norway. Working with kids takes a lot of personality and patience, and the number of "junior cruisers" is growing each year.

ships now offer free seasickness medication at the Purser's Desk and doctor's office. If you have a history of motion sickness, you may want to consider a doctor-prescribed patch that is placed behind your ear. Chances are you won't have a problem anyway. If you're sailing in the Caribbean, you are in a sea, not the ocean; the water does not get that rough. The same is true of cruises to Alaska, where you sail on an inside waterway, for the most part insulated from the storms of the Pacific Ocean.

Homesickness is not so easily cured. If you've attended an out-of-state college or worked in a city away from home, you may be better prepared for life on a ship than the average person. The main difference is that there is almost no chance of your being able to see family or friends for the length of your employment. You'll be on the ship from three months to a year. You'll be making new friends, who will soon be as close as family, but no one can replace your parents, good friends, or a special person you were dating back home. You have to decide if you want to give that up temporarily. You'll have fun on the ship, no doubt. But you won't be able to go out to a new movie, you won't get to see your favorite ball team play, and you probably won't be home for your birthday or Christmas. Decide which is more important to you, and whether the trade-off is worth it.

What do I have to offer the cruise lines? You can be the most persistent person on earth in your application efforts; yet if you don't have valuable qualifications to offer, you are not going to be hired. You have to ask yourself, "Am I applying because I could do a great job or because I just want to go on a cruise ship and party?" If the answer is to party, even if you are hired, you won't last long. You must be applying for the right reasons, giving the cruise lines something to gain, or you won't have a chance.

How committed am I? We have seen that getting a job on a cruise ship is not easy. You would need some extraordinary qualifications to be able to apply, get an offer, and walk on a ship. You're much more likely to encounter standard rejection letters and people who don't return your calls. How you react to those disappointments will determine whether or not you end up with a job. If you're committed to getting that job and you are qualified, you'll keep applying and staying in contact with the right people until you get exactly what you want—a job on board a ship!

Is It the Right Job for You?

Princess Cruise Line's Royal Princess *visits one of its many exotic ports of call.*

> Friends for Life
> The most rewarding part of shipboard life is the relationships you build, the friends you make.
> Because ships are so confined, you must get along with everyone. You are around both crew members and passengers all day and night. The time is so "condensed" that it allows you to grow close in the span of a couple of days.
> One family I met became like an adoptive family to me. We corresponded frequently after their first cruise, a ten-day trip to the Caribbean. Every summer after that, they planned their vacation around my schedule and took a cruise on whichever ship I was working. One year, on my vacation, they even flew me to their home in Texas.

> I could never have established such close ties to people in a nightclub on land. I am still friends with most of the people I met on the ships, and I have pen pals all over the world.
>
> Juliann Pugh

Appendix A
Cruise Ship Ports of Call Around the World

CARIBBEAN
Key West, Florida
San Juan, Puerto Rico
St. Thomas, U.S. Virgin Islands
St. John, U.S. Virgin Islands
St. Croix, U.S. Virgin Islands
Tortola, British Virgin Islands
Virgin Gorda, British Virgin Islands
Philipsburg, St. Maarten
St. Johns, Antigua
Basseterre, St. Kitts
Kingstown, St. Vincent
Castries, St. Lucia
Puerto Plata, Dominican Republic
Roseau, Dominica
Gustavia, St. Barts
Point-a-Pitre, Guadeloupe
Fort-de-France, Martinique
Bridgetown, Barbados
Montego Bay, Jamaica
Ocho Rios, Jamaica
Georgetown, Grand Cayman
Port of Spain, Trinidad

Willemstad, Curaçao
Oranjestad, Aruba

EAST COAST OF MEXICO
Cancun
Playa del Carmen
Cozumel

BAHAMAS
Nassau
Freeport
Stirrup Cay
Abacos Out Islands

PANAMA CANAL
St. Georges, Costa Rica
Caldera, Costa Rica
San Blas Islands

SOUTH AMERICA
Valparaiso (Santiago), Chile
Buenos Aires, Argentina
Montevideo, Uruguay
Amazon River
Orinoco River
Fortaleza, Brazil
São Paulo, Brazil
Manaus, Brazil
Salvador, Brazil
Recife, Brazil
Rio de Janeiro, Brazil
Cartagena, Colombia
Devil's Island, French Guiana
Caracas, Venezuela
La Guaira, Venezuela

Appendix A

West Coast of Mexico
Ixtapa
Mazatlan
Manzanillo
Zihuatanejo
Cabo San Lucas
Puerto Vallarta
Acapulco

Canada, Alaska, West Coast of U.S.
Victoria, British Columbia
Vancouver, British Columbia
Prince Rupert, British Columbia
Port Hardy, Alaska
Haines, Alaska
Skagway, Alaska
Ketchikan, Alaska
Sitka, Alaska
Anchorage, Alaska
Homer, Alaska
Seward, Alaska
Wrangell, Alaska
Glacier Bay
Misty Fjords
Seattle, Washington
Portland, Oregon
Ensenada, California
Catalina Island, California
San Francisco, California
Los Angeles, California
San Diego, California

Hawaii
Honolulu
Lahaina

Oahu
Kauai
Kona
Hilo
Maui

SOUTH PACIFIC
Pago Pago, American Samoa
Moorea, French Polynesia
Bora Bora, French Polynesia
Tahiti, French Polynesia
Marquesas Islands, French Polynesia
Wellington, New Zealand
Auckland, New Zealand
Brisbane, Australia
Cairns, Australia
Sydney, Australia
Melbourne, Australia
Perth, Australia
Manila, Philippine Islands
Bali, Indonesia

FAR EAST
Bombay, India
Maldive Islands
Kuala Lumpur, Malaysia
Bangkok, Thailand
Pusan, Korea
Seoul, Korea
Singapore
Hong Kong
Shanghai, China
Nanjing, China
Dalian, China
Taipei, Taiwan
Kobe, Japan

Appendix A

Nagasaki, Japan
Okinawa, Japan

Mediterranean
Istanbul, Turkey
Kusadasi, Turkey
Corfu, Greece
Mykonos, Greece
Athens (Piraeus), Greece
Rhodes, Greece
Dubrovnik, Yugoslavia
Haifa, Israel
Port Said, Egypt
Alexandria, Egypt
Tunis, Tunisia
Capri, Italy
Messina, Italy
Portofino, Italy
Venice, Italy
Naples, Italy
Civitavecchia (Rome), Italy
Corsica, France
Villefranche (Nice, Monte Carlo), France
St. Tropez, France
Palma de Mallorca, Spain
Malaga, Spain
Barcelona, Spain
Gibraltar
Tangier, Morocco
Casablanca, Morocco

Europe
Hamburg, Germany
Paris, France
Kiel, Germany
Edinburgh, Scotland

Waterford, Ireland
Cork, Ireland

SCANDINAVIA
Helsinki, Finland
Stockholm, Sweden
Visby, Sweden
Copenhagen, Denmark
Oslo, Norway
Bergen, Norway
Trondheim, Norway
Gdansk, Poland
Reykjavik, Iceland

CANARY ISLANDS (TRANSATLANTIC)
Tenerife
Las Palmas
Lanzarote

BERMUDA
Somerset
St. Georges
Hamilton

CANADA/NEW ENGLAND
Saguenay Fjord
Cape Cod Canal
Prince Edward Island
Montreal, Quebec
Halifax, Nova Scotia
Sydney, Nova Scotia
Bar Harbor, Maine
Boston, Massachusetts
Newport, Rhode Island
New York, New York

APPENDIX A

U.S. RIVERS
Pittsburgh, Pennsylvania
Cincinnati, Ohio
Louisville, Kentucky
Minneapolis/St. Paul, Minnesota
St. Louis, Missouri
Chattanooga, Tennessee
Nashville, Tennessee
Memphis, Tennessee
Baton Rouge, Louisiana
New Orleans, Louisiana

EAST COAST OF U.S.
Miami, Florida
Port Everglades, Florida
Port Canaveral, Florida
Ft. Lauderdale, Florida
West Palm Beach, Florida
Jacksonville, Florida
Savannah, Georgia
Charleston, South Carolina
Washington, D.C.
Baltimore, Maryland
Annapolis, Maryland
Norfolk, Virginia
Philadelphia, Pennsylvania

Appendix B
Commonly Asked Questions About Cruise Vacations

The following is a reprint of the CLIA's brochure distributed to potential cruisers by travel agents around the country.* Some of the questions have been discussed in detail in the book; others were mentioned only briefly. Knowing the answers will help you to understand the shipboard environment and the concerns of the people you are being hired to serve.

Isn't cruising expensive?
There are cruise vacations to suit every budget, from the cost-conscious to the most luxurious. Even more important, a cruise offers the best travel value for your money. Your fare includes all meals, your stateroom, on board daytime activities, nighttime parties, and entertainment. So for once, you'll know what your vacation will cost you before you go. (Your only extra expenses will be drinks, optional shore excursions, and personal services such as massages or hairstyling.)

How long are cruises?
As long, or short, as you want. CLIA's member lines offer itineraries from three days to three months.

---

* Reprinted with permission.

Can I book on short notice?
Even the most popular cruise ships sometimes have space available because of late cancellations. Have your travel agent check. But to get exactly the ship, cabin, and sailing date you want, you should plan and book early.

How do I book a cruise?
See your CLIA travel agent! This professional will help you pick the cruise that fits your vacation schedule, tastes, and budget and then make all the arrangements to get you from your doorstep to your stateroom.

Are all ships and cruises fairly similar?
Far from it. CLIA member lines' ships range from under 200 feet to over 1,000. You can sail with fewer than 100 fellow passengers to nearly 2,500. Experience atmospheres ranging from casual to formal, classically simple to ultra-deluxe. You can even choose between propeller-driven craft and sailing ships.

What's an air/sea cruise?
A "fly/cruise" or an "air/sea cruise" package includes either free or much reduced airfare along with your cruise ticket. These money-saving options include transfers between the airport and ship as well as baggage handling.

Do I need a passport?
This depends on the type of cruise and your destination. You'll probably need, at least, some proof of citizenship. You'll receive complete information on required documents well in advance of your departure so you'll have plenty of time to make arrangements.

Are there different classes of service?
Today's cruise ships are "one-class." Everyone on board can use all of the ship's facilities. The price of a stateroom is based only on its size and location. Regardless of the category you book, you'll enjoy the same service, menus, activities, and entertainment as everyone else on board.

Will I get bored? Feel confined?
Hardly. Being at sea gives you a feeling of freedom few places can offer. There's plenty of room. It'll probably take you two or three days just to discover what's on board, plus you get the added adventure of exploring exciting ports of call.

Cruise ships are like floating resorts. You can be by yourself and lie back in a lounge chair, breathe in the sea air, soak up the sun, read good books, or watch the ever-changing view. Or you can join in exercise classes, dance classes, sports contests, and other organized deck activities. Perhaps you can practice your tennis strokes, drive golf balls, shoot some skeet or basketballs. You can go for a swim, stretch out in the sauna, or work out in the gym. You can see a feature movie, attend lectures by renowned experts, play backgammon or bridge. And that's just when you're on board!

What's there to do in port?
So much, you'll have a hard time choosing! You can go off on your own or take a guided tour. You can search ancient ruins or hunt shopping bargains. Ride a raft over river rapids, a bicycle down the side of a 10,000-foot volcano, or a horse across miles of hills and beaches. Climb a waterfall or a pyramid. See the birthplace of civilization or steel drum bands. Follow the footsteps of history or the wake of a waterskiing boat.

If there's still time (and you aren't ready to rest yet),

enjoy a folkloric show. Play golf or tennis. Eat native foods. Learn how to windsurf. Sun and swim at some of the world's best beaches. Catch a record marlin. Sail, snorkel, or go scuba diving. Go to a nightclub or glittering casino. Take a cable car to the top of a mountain. Explore dark catacombs.

In short, a cruise is the easiest way to see new places and do all the things you've dreamed of.

Do I have to participate in the activities?
On a cruise you do what you want to do. You can do everything or lie back and do absolutely nothing. It's your vacation.

Do cruise lines welcome families with kids?
Twenty-five percent of cruise vacations are booked by families with children. Most cruise lines provide supervised activities for youngsters, especially during school holidays. If your children enjoy swimming, sports, games, movies, and the adventure of new places, they'll love a family cruise. You'll find that kids adapt to shipboard life with ease, and you won't have to wonder what they're up to every minute. The cruise staff will help keep them busy and entertained. Best of all, children generally travel at a substantially reduced rate.

What's there to do at night?
At night, life aboard a cruise ship really turns on. There's dancing, live entertainment in the nightclubs, discos, and lounges. Feature films. And parties with all your new friends. Most ships even have casinos. There are also many special events, like the Captain's Cocktail Party, the passengers' talent night, the Masquerade Parade, the Midnight Buffet (for one last bite to tide you over till breakfast). The night can go on as long as you want. Even until the spectacle of sunrise at sea.

Is there a charge for the entertainment?
Never. On a cruise vacation, the entertainment is on the house. There's no cover. No minimum. No admission charge. The shows are live. The movies are first-rate. The variety is limitless.

Is it easy to meet people?
A cruise ship is a great place to make new friends, because everyone's so friendly. The atmosphere is cordial, relaxed. And you'll have all kinds of things in common to talk about. At dinner. At cocktails. Around the pool. Or along the promenade rail. Don't be surprised if you find yourself making arrangements to meet them aboard ship again next year.

Will there be people like me?
No matter what you've heard to the contrary, there's no such thing as a typical cruise passenger. All kinds of people take cruises... of all ages... from all walks of life... singles, couples, and families. Passengers can vary from ship to ship and cruise to cruise. Ask your CLIA travel agent for advice on the best ship for you, your tastes, and your life-style.

Can singles have fun on a cruise?
Cruising is ideal for people traveling alone because it's so easy to meet people. In fact, most ships have parties just for singles—early on, so you can become involved right away. Most ships also have single cabins as well as single rates for double staterooms. In many cases, a cruise line will even find you a roommate to share a double if you ask them.

What should I pack?
Pack as you would for any resort. Cruise vacations are casual by day, whether you're on the ship or ashore. In

the evening, the dress code varies. As on shore, attire is dictated by occasion. For the Captain's Gala, for example, you'll probably want to wear something more formal, such as a dark suit or cocktail dress; perhaps even a dinner jacket or gown.

Will I need a tuxedo?
On some cruises, formal dinners or parties are part of the fun. But don't buy a tux just for the trip. Even on the most formal of ships, a dark suit and tie are fine for the dressiest occasions.

Can I use my hairdryer or shaver?
Most ships have 110-volt outlets in the staterooms. But do check with your CLIA travel agent to be sure.

What are "different meal seatings?"
Some ship's dining rooms can accommodate all passengers in one "seating." But most ships have two seatings, which differ only by time. Decide whether you prefer to dine early or later, then have your travel agent request your preference when you book. Whichever seating you choose, remember that one of the best ways to make new friends is to ask for a large table.

Can I have seconds?
Everything you've ever heard about cruise ship dining is true. You'll find a varied selection of entrees (appetizers, salads, soups, vegetables, and desserts, too) every time you sit down. And there's virtually no limit to what or how much you can order. Best of all, the one thing you'll never see on a cruise ship menu is a price!

What about fitness and healthy eating?
Just because your cruise ship offers plenty of delicious food doesn't mean you'll come home out of shape. You can

choose "low-cal" or "fitness" selections that are just as tempting as the regular menu. You can also jog, do aerobics, work out in the gym, swim, golf, play tennis, and much more. Burning calories was never so much fun!

Can I get a special diet?
Most ships can accommodate salt-free, low-carbohydrate, kosher, or other diet preferences. However, this request must be made in advance.

What if I don't like my tablemates?
Rarely is this a problem. However if you wish to move to another table, speak with the maitre d'. He'll make every effort to seat you with more compatible dining companions . . . discreetly and politely.

Are there nonsmoking areas?
Today, virtually all ships have smoking and nonsmoking tables and/or sections in the dining rooms and lounges. If you want your dining table in a nonsmoking area, tell your travel agent. On board, in "open-seating" situations, you can advise your waiter or the maitre d'.

Can we celebrate a special day?
Absolutely! Most cruise lines will even treat you to a complimentary cake and a chorus of "Happy Whatever" to honor the occasion. Your birthday or anniversary can be more festive with champagne, flowers, canapés, wine, or cheese. You can even arrange for a special private party. All you have to do is advise your travel agent in advance.

Is cruising right for honeymooners?
Without a doubt. Cruising creates an atmosphere that's just right for romance . . . cozy dinners for two, strolling on deck at sunset, dancing the night away (even under

the stars), and so much more to remember forever. Most lines provide special services, from Sunday or Monday departures to welcome champagne and breakfast in bed. (And, speaking of beds, most ships have them in double, queen, or king sizes!)

Can we stay in touch with the "outside"?
Quite easily. Most ships have a daily newsletter with news headlines, selected stock quotes, and sports scores. You can call someone on shore through the ship's radio operator while at sea. And you can make phone calls from most ports of call.

What about tipping?
Tipping is a matter of individual preference. A general rule of thumb is to plan for about $2.50 to $3.00 per person per day for your room steward and dining room waiter, and about half that amount for your busboy. (A few cruise lines include tipping in the price and will so inform you.) Other shipboard personnel can be tipped for special services at your discretion.

Isn't motion discomfort a problem?
Not really. The most popular cruise areas boast some of the calmest waters in the world. In addition, stabilizers on modern ships, advance availability of accurate weather information, and development of effective preventive medications have, for the most part, eliminated the incidence of motion discomfort.

Are there medical services on board?
Virtually every cruise ship (except for some smaller vessels operating in coastal waters) has a fully equipped medical facility and staff to handle almost any emergency.

Are there laundry services aboard?
Yes. Almost all cruise ships have laundry facilities, and a great many provide dry-cleaning services. There is, however, an additional charge for professional laundry and dry-cleaning services. Most ships also have self-service laundries.

Do cruise lines accept group bookings?
Most lines work with groups, often at reduced rates, depending on the number of people. Policies vary from company to company and sometimes during certain times of the year. Consult with your travel agent for details.

Are there meeting rooms on board?
Just about every full-size ship has public rooms to offer as meeting space for groups. Ask your travel agent to contact the cruise line's group sales department to coordinate schedules and arrange for any catering needs. Your ship may also be able to offer audiovisual equipment.

Can I extend my cruise vacation?
Your travel agent can arrange pre- or post-cruise land packages at the time you book your cruise. In many cases, your airline ticket includes helpful options, such as free stopovers, that enable you to make your own special arrangements.

It all sounds too good to be true! Is it?
In all seriousness, the one major complaint we hear over and over again is that cruises end far too soon! Beyond that, it's hard to find any negatives. After all, you don't have to run to make plane connections to get from one port to the next. You don't have the hassles of making dinner or nightclub reservations. You don't have the

bother of packing and unpacking as you move from place to place. You don't get expensive surprises at restaurants or nightclubs. You have a wealth of options for shopping, adventure, sightseeing, exploring, entertainment, and sports activities. All you have to worry about is relaxing and enjoying your vacation.

Whom should I see if I have other questions?
Check the Yellow Pages for your nearest CLIA-Affiliated Travel Agent, designated by the CLIA seal. With nearly 20,000 such agencies nationwide, there's one close by! These travel professionals are knowledgeable about all the options available for your cruise experience. In fact, you'll find that most have been on cruises, so they can advise you from personal experience.

Glossary

ASTA American Society of Travel Agents.
berth A bed on a ship.
booking A reservation with a cruise line to take a cruise on a specified date.
bow The front of the ship.
bridge The operational, navigational, and communications center of the ship, located on a top deck at the bow of the ship.
cabin A "room" on a ship.
Captain's table Table in the dining room where the ship's Captain and his invited guests dine.
CLIA Cruise Lines International Association.
concessionaire Outside company that operates a department or provides employees for a department on a cruise ship.
crew The working staff of a cruise ship.
cruise fare The cost of a cruise, paid upfront, which includes airfare and transfers, all meals, cabin, and on board activities and entertainment.
deck A floor or level of a ship.
dinner sitting Specific time a group of passengers have meals (usually half at an early sitting, the other half two hours later).
disembark To get off the ship.
double A cabin with berths for two people.
draft Depth at which the ship's hull sits in the water.
duty-free Available for sale with no special taxes added to the purchase price.
embark To go aboard a ship.

GLOSSARY

foreign exchange rate   Rate at which U.S. dollars may be exchanged for foreign currency in ports.
formal night   A specially designated night or nights when dress code is cocktail dresses for ladies and tuxedo or dark suit for men.
galley   The ship's kitchen areas.
gangway   The flat or stepped walkway lowered from the side of the ship to allow passengers to embark and disembark.
host program   Older men who work on the ship as dining and dancing companions for elderly women sailing alone.
itinerary   The planned list of ports a ship visits during a cruise.
knot   One nautical mile per hour (6,080 feet).
maiden voyage   The first sailing of a new ship.
off-season   The time of year when the fewest people are taking cruises and prices are lower.
passenger manifest   List of all passengers on board a cruise.
passenger talent show   Event held on most large ships giving passengers the chance to compete for prizes or money.
port   The left side of the ship looking toward the front.
ports of call   The specific cities or resorts that cruise ships visit.
port tax   Fee charged by the cruise ship's home port for each passenger boarding there.
private island   A small tropical island owned by a cruise line that serves as a private port of call, providing music, outdoor buffets, and beach and watersports activities.
Purser's Desk   The on-board office where passengers may register complaints, store valuables, or exchange money (equivalent of front desk at a hotel).
quad   A cabin with four berths.

repositioning cruise Short port-to-port cruise to change itineraries (may or may not have passengers aboard).

shore excursion An organized tour in a port of call, usually sold on board before arriving at the port).

single A cabin capable of sleeping two people but occupied by only one.

stabilizers Nautical devices that extend from the hull of a ship to reduce rocking or bouncing in rough seas.

starboard The right side of the ship looking toward the front.

steel band Type of music usually provided on ships sailing to ports in the Caribbean.

stern/aft The back or rear of the ship.

suite Larger cabin usually offering a king-size bed or full-size bathroom and other extra amenities.

table assignment The specific table at which a passenger sits for all meals.

tenders Small boats, usually the ship's lifeboats, used to take passengers to shore in ports where the ship cannot dock.

terminal The large building housing ticket counters, tourist shops, and pay phones at which a cruise ship docks.

theme cruise Cruise having entertainment and activities highlighted by a general theme such as big band music, sports stars, or a murder mystery.

transfers Transportation to and from the airport and the cruise ship terminal.

triple A cabin with three berths.

visitor's pass Hard-to-get permission from the cruise line for a nonpassenger to visit the ship while in port.

wake The churned water a ship leaves in its path as it sails forward.

For Further Reading

Bannerman, Gary. *Bon Voyage—The Cruise Traveler's Handbook.* Lincolnwood, IL: National Textbook Company, 1985.
Blum, Ethel. *The Total Traveler by Ship.* Surfside, FL: 1989.
Cairis, Nicholas T. *Cruise Ships of the World.* Cambridge, MA: Pegasus Books, 1989.
DeLand, Antoinette. *Fielding's Worldwide Cruises.* New York: William Morrow and Company, 1988.
Grant, Edgar. *Exploring Careers in the Travel Industry.* New York: Rosen Publishing Group, 1989.
Kennedy, Don. *How to Get a Job on a Cruise Ship.* Atlanta: CareerSouth Publications, 1991.
Maltzman, Jeff. *Jobs in Paradise. The Definitive Guide to Exotic Jobs Everywhere.* New York: HarperCollins, 1990.
Maritime Services Directory. San Diego: Aegis Publications, 1989.
Springer, Marylyn. *Frommer's Cruises 1991–92.* New York: Prentice-Hall Press, 1991.
Ward, Douglas. *Berlitz Complete Handbook of Cruising.* New York: Macmillan, 1991.

Periodicals:
Cruise Magazine, Gulf Breeze, Florida.
Cruise Travel, Evanston, Illinois.

Index

A
activities
　aerobics, 11, 27
　dancing, 4, 9, 11, 21, 57
　entertainment, 4
　gambling, 4, 11
　games, 12
　golf, 12
　jogging, 12
　sightseeing, 13, 18
　sports, 7, 9, 12–13, 27
　sunbathing, 3, 13, 57
　swimming, 13
adventure, spirit of, 50
age limits, cruise staff, 43–44
Alaska, 4, 18, 28, 32, 34, 67–68, 84–85, 90–95, 98, 101, 130
Amazon River, 28
American Hawaii Cruises, 27, 56, 69–70
American crews, 2, 45, 56, 58–59
appearance, importance of, 51, 126
application, job, 49, 105
　formal, 113
　follow-up, 115–120
　photo for, 113–114
attitude, importance of, 50, 125–126

B
Bahamas, 4, 6, 32, 67, 68, 71–73, 83, 85–87, 89–91, 95
Barbados, 23, 35
Barefoot Cruises, 17, 29
bar manager, 65
bartender, 1, 2, 44, 65
beautician, 44, 69, 101
Bermuda, 4, 21, 73, 78–79, 86, 93–94

big band, 9, 27
brevity, of cover letter, 106, 107
British crew, 2

C
cabin arrangements, 2, 9, 16, 17, 33, 58, 130, 138–139
Canada, 34, 77–78, 91–92, 96
Caribbean Sea, 4, 18, 23, 26, 28, 46, 54, 67, 68, 71, 73–79, 82, 84–88, 90–95, 97–98, 100, 130, 133
Carnival Cruise Lines, 3, 4, 26, 30–31, 48, 68, 70–71, 84, 135–136
casino, 11–12, 44, 58, 101–102
　staff, 63
Celebration, 70
Chandris Celebrity Cruises, 26, 30, 73
Chandris Fantasy Cruises, 73
children, programs for, 6, 20, 27–28, 30, 57, 145
classes, educational, 12
climate, choice of, 34
clothes, for cruise ship job, 130–131
Club Med, 29, 74–75
commitment, 37, 53, 147
Commodore Cruise Line, 75–76
competition, beating, 37–40
concessions, 69, 101–103
correspondence, follow-up by, 117–118
CostaClassica, 27
Costa Cruise Line, 26, 27, 76–77
couples, 6, 21
cover letter, 105–108, 117
Cramer, Douglas, 1

171

INDEX

Crown Cruise Line, 77–78
Crown Princess, 24, 39
cruise director, 1, 2, 11, 22, 40, 61
cruise industry, 3, 23–36
   trends in, 26–31
Cruise Line Directory, 67–104
Cruise Line International Association, 31, 34–35
cruise ship
   staff, 55, 56–59, 61, 125, 130
      life of, 138–143
   types of, 1–3
cruises
   sailing, 29
   types of, 3–4
cruise to nowhere, 3–4, 20
Crystal Cruises, 30, 78
Cunard Line, 26, 31, 78–80

D

dancers, 9, 62
deck and engine staff, 55, 59
Delta Queen Steamboat Company, 27, 56, 80–81
Diamond Cruise, 81–82
Diana, Princess, 24
dining room
   cruise staff, 56, 58, 139
   officers', 42, 56, 139
disco, 21, 57
DJ, 9, 21–22, 57, 62
doctor, 1, 64, 142, 146
Dolphin Cruise Line, 82–83
Dorn, Amy, 14, 103–104
dressing up, 8, 11
drug use, 40, 142
Dutch crews, 84

E

Ecstasy, 48
education, 44, 58
educational cruises, 26–27
Effjohn International, 75, 77
empathy, 51
entertainer, 62, 99–100, 135–136
   headline, 57

entertainment, 9, 57, 102
Epirotiki Lines, 26, 83–84
Europe, 67, 73–75, 77–79, 88, 91, 95–96
experience, work, 58, 106

F

facilities, sports/fitness, 27
families, 6, 21, 24, 27, 30
Fantasy, 4
Far East, 18, 67, 79, 87–91, 98
flexibility, of hours, 52
food and beverage staff, 44, 55, 56, 59–60, 102–103, 141
formal dress, 16–17, 130
format, cover-letter
   chronological, 110–113
   functional, 109–110
four-day cruises, 4, 20, 30, 32
friends
   cruising with, 24
   making, 13, 138, 147

G

Gifford, Kathy Lee, 3
Greece, 76–77, 83–84, 88, 93
Greek crews, 2, 56, 60, 95, 98

H

Hawaii, 28, 90–92, 95–96
health, as requirement, 43, 58
Hepburn, Audrey, 24
Holland America Line, 26, 30, 84–85
homesickness, 38, 144–146
honeymooners, 6, 30
hostess, cruise ship, 61
"host," gentlemen, 6
hotel staff, 44, 55, 59, 64, 141
hours, working, 141
humor, sense of, 50
hurricane, encounter with, 35–36

I

Indonesian crews, 84
interview, job, 105, 121–128

INDEX

Island Princess, 1
island, private, 18, 85, 132
Italian crews, 2, 56, 60
itinerary, 18, 28, 33, 68, 130, 141

J
Jamaican crewmember, 2
job
    applying for, 105–114
    accepting, 129
    assessing suitability for, 144–147
    market, 37–42
    offer of, 116–117
jobs available, 55–66

K
Kelley, Suzanne, 53–54, 119–120, 125
Kennedy, Don, 21–22, 35–36, 111–113
Kloster Cruise Limited, 31, 96

L
language, foreign, 41–42, 44–46, 67, 103–104
Loren, Sophia, 24
"Love Boat, The," 1–2, 8, 35, 90
luck, as quality, 49

M
MacLeod, Gavin, 1
maître d'hôtel, 65
Majesty Cruise Line, 30, 85
massage, 7, 12, 27, 45, 69, 101
masseuse, 63
meals, 3, 8, 9, 11, 24, 32
    buffet, 7, 9, 10
    consumption at, 24
    diet, 7, 19–20
Mediterranean Sea, 4, 18, 26, 67, 75–79, 82–84, 88, 91, 93–95, 97–98, 100, 133
megaliners, 28, 39
Mexico, 4, 23, 26, 67, 71–76, 84–86, 90–96
Mississippi River, 34, 81

movies, 7, 12
musician, staff, 62
myths and misconceptions, cruise, 15–21

N
New England, 34, 77–78, 91–92
Norway, 27, 145
Norwegian Cruise Line, xiii, 26, 27, 85–87, 96, 132
Norwegians, 2, 56, 60
notice of sailing, short, 51–52, 129
nurse, staff, 64, 142

O
Oceanic Cruises, 87–88
officers, 43, 55, 56, 141

P
Pacific Princess, 1
packing
    for sailing, 130–135
    and unpacking, 7
pampering, 7, 8, 24, 46
Panama Canal, 26, 82, 84–85, 90–92, 94–96
P and O, 31, 90
Paquet French Cruises, 88–89
passengers
    age of, 5, 30, 31–32, 68
    types of, 5–6, 17–18
passport, 16
patience, as quality, 51
people skills, 46, 49–50, 144
persistence, as quality, 37, 53, 119
personality, outgoing, 46, 106–107, 126
photographer, staff, 58, 64, 102
photography, 13, 131
ports of call, 4, 18, 21, 27, 28, 33, 141, 149–155
Premier Cruise Lines, 28, 29, 89
price, value for, 7, 8–13, 15, 32–33
Princess Cruise Line, 1, 24, 26, 31, 68, 90–91, 148
privacy, lack of, 52

INDEX

promotion, 40, 56
public speaking, 50
Pugh, Juliann, 66, 99–100, 135–136, 141
purser, 1, 40–42, 56, 64
Purser's Desk, 20, 40–42, 146

Q

qualifications, 37, 43–45, 106, 146
qualities, personal, 49–53
questions, commonly asked, 156–165

R

Radisson Diamond, 29
reasons for cruising, 7–8
recreation/fitness director, 11, 14, 58, 61
Regal Princess, 24, 39
Regency Cruises, 91–92
rejection letter, 116, 147
religious services, 143
Renaissance, 28
Renaissance Cruises, 26, 92–93
résumé, 46, 105–106, 108–113, 117
retail staff, 58, 63, 102–103
romance, 1, 6, 8, 13
Royal Caribbean Cruise Line, 26, 30–31, 53, 93–95
Royal Cruise Line, 95–96
Royal Princess, 1, 24, 148
Royal Viking Line, 30, 96
Royal Viking Queen, 30, 96

S

salaries, 61–66
 payment of, 139
satisfaction rating, 23, 24
Scandinavia, 88, 96, 130
scuba diving, 131, 134
 instructor, 63
Seabourn Cruise Line, 30, 96–97
Sea Goddess, 28
seasickness, 20, 144–146
Seaward, xiii, 128

Seawind Cruise Line, 97
seven-day cruises, 4, 6
Seven Seas Cruise Line, 97–98
ships
 new, 26, 28, 30, 40
 size of, 32
shopping, 7, 12, 33
shore excursion director, 61
shows, Broadway-style, 8, 9, 11, 24, 57
singles (unmarried), 6, 21, 30
singles (traveling alone), 6, 18
Sitmar Cruise Line, 113
shills, key, 46–49
Sky Princess, 1
snorkeling, 13, 131, 134
Song of America, 53
South America, 18, 73–74, 78, 82, 88, 90–92, 95, 98, 133
South Pacific, 4, 74–75, 78, 89, 90, 97, 100, 133
Spelling, Aaron, 1
sport director, 103–104
Star Princess, 24
steward
 chief, 64
 room, 59, 64, 141
 wine, 66
stress, handling, 50
sunglasses, 133–134
Sun Line Cruises, 98
Sun Viking, 53
Swedish crew, 2

T

technician, sound/light, 57, 72
telephone
 follow-up by, 117–118
 interview by, 121–123
termination, involuntary, 40, 49, 142
Thatcher, Margaret, 24
theme cruises, 27, 85–86
three-day cruises, 4, 6, 20, 30
tips (gratuities), 59, 97, 98, 139
tips

INDEX

on personal interview, 125–127
on preparing cover letter, 106–107
transportation, 7–8, 9, 16
travel agent, 5, 15, 31–34
tuxedo, 16, 130

U
uniforms, 130–131, 136–137
United States, 85, 86, 91

W
waiters, 59, 65, 141
Walt Disney World, 28, 29, 89
Windstar Cruises, 29, 30, 100
women, elderly, on cruises, 6
world cruises, 4, 68, 78–79, 84, 96, 97
World Explorer, 100–101

Y
youth coordinator, 61–62, 119–120

9/23/94